Murder at Cherry Hill

Murder At Cherry Hill

The Strang-Whipple Case, 1827

LOUIS C. JONES

Introduction by
THEODORE CORBETT

Drawings by
RON TOELKE

HISTORIC CHERRY HILL
Albany, New York

A Cherry Hill Publication

For
Aggie

Contents

LOUIS C. JONES was born in 1908 in Albany, where his father was Superintendent of Schools. Educated at Albany High School, Hamilton College (B.A.), and Columbia University (M.A. and Ph.D.), he taught English and folklore for twelve years at the New York State College for Teachers, the predecessor of the State University of New York in Albany. In 1946 he was appointed Director of the New York State Historical Association and its Farmer's Museum; during the twenty-five years of his directorship the Seminars on American Culture and the Cooperstown Graduate Programs were initiated, the Farmer's Museum tripled in size and the famous folk-art collection was acquired and researched. Dr. Jones is a Guggenheim Fellow and has received the George McAneny Award, the American Association of State and Local History's Award of Distinction, and the Northeast Museum Conference's Katherine Coffee Award. With Harold W. Thompson, he founded the New York Folklore Society and was the first editor of its *Quarterly*. He is currently Adjunct Professor of Folk Art at the Cooperstown Graduate Programs.

THEODORE CORBETT, Director of Historic Cherry Hill, has a Ph.D. in history and has written widely on early American social history and material culture.

RON TOELKE, partner of Flash Graphics of Chatham, New York, has illustrated the *Kent Family Chronicles Encyclopedia* and recently received a national award for one of the best paperback covers of 1980.

List of Illustrations

Preface

FOR nearly fifty years now I have been intrigued by how much social history lies buried in accounts of murder trials and in the confessions of murderers. In this regard few can match the trials of Jesse Strang and Elsie Lansing Whipple. Here are insights to the patterns and taboos of class, to slavery, to the impact of canals, to the irritations of travel. (The trunk that went to New York instead of Albany, and when one turned up it was not at all the one that was lost, causes the air traveler to smile sadly.) Here are questions about the rights and lack of rights of women of property, about wages and prices and currency itself, about crime and dramatized punishment, about the courts and the Establishment.

The case is so provocative that in 1977 my colleague Dr. Langdon Wright and I offered a research seminar at the Cooperstown Graduate Programs using it as a

11

basis for dealing with such matters as genealogy, surrogate's records, the law, architecture of Cherry Hill and especially women in nineteenth-century Albany. This manuscript was already at hand and some of the very able young women in the class felt I had treated Elsie unfairly. Since then I have reviewed the evidence but I have not changed my mind. I have seldom had a class I enjoyed more; on May 7, 1977 they had a sesquicentennial party to commemorate the murder, serving food from Cherry Hill's *Selected Receipts of a Van Rensselaer Family* and indulging in a series of happy, macabre pranks.

My acknowledgments must go back many years, first to the late John Scopes and his brother Frank, bookmen extraordinary, who found my first copies of the *Trial of Jesse Strang* and the *Confession* in the early '30s. The manuscript was first written in the '60s and typed and retyped by my able, long-suffering secretary, Margie Willsey. I was delighted a few years ago when Cornelia Frisbee Houde, then Director of Historic Cherry Hill, suggested that some time her institution would like to publish this monograph and delighted again when her successor, Dr. Theodore Corbett, was able to bring it to pass. To a native Albanian, born no farther away from Cherry Hill than lower Madison Avenue, it seems very neighborly, a kind of homecoming in print.

In recent years since I brought the manuscript out of mothballs, a number of people have read it and made suggestions, notably Dr. Bruce T. Sherwood and Professor Langdon Wright and the students in our seminar: Anthony Cucchiara, Leigh Jones, Sheila McDonald,

Stacy Fox Pomeroy, who the next year made major contributions to the *Historic Structure Report of Cherry Hill,* J.R. Phillips, Dorothy Routh, James Ryan, Elizabeth Sharpe. Another year we also had as a student Jane Carpenter Kellar who had been one of the editors of the book of Van Rensselaer recipes.

The staff at Historic Cherry Hill have been most helpful in preparing the manuscript for publication: Leo Wong has been a patient and efficient editor; Maxine Lorang has checked my facts and saved me embarrassment. Stacy Fox Pomeroy and Douglas G. Bucher have served as the staff's architectural consultants. But especially my gratitude goes to Dr. Theodore Corbett not only for his valuable Introduction, but for the understanding and cooperative spirit he has shown throughout this venture.

Finally the gratitude that is beyond expressing to my partner, Agnes Halsey Jones.

L.C.J.

Cooperstown, N.Y.
June 1982

Introduction

BY THEODORE CORBETT
DIRECTOR OF HISTORIC CHERRY HILL

THE account you are about to read concerns a love affair that culminates in a murder—the ingredients of a Hollywood thriller. Those of you who enjoy a story of popular passion will not be disappointed, but in addition you will find this an exciting piece of social history. In fact, the study of murders provides us with some of our most vivid and accurate descriptions of the human condition. The need for such accounts was demonstrated to Historic Cherry Hill at a 1981 conference cosponsored by us on Early Hudson Valley Families. We discovered that little work had been done on the Hudson Valley's nineteenth-century social history. In our opinion, Louis C. Jones' account of the murder at Cherry Hill is a landmark in the study of the region's social history and as such will serve as a starting point for further investigation of this neglected aspect of our history.

The setting for the murder is the Albany of the 1820s, an era that is not easy for us to come to grips with. Some historians like to have us think that after the Revolutionary War there was a rapid vindication of republican institutions, that democracy and industrial free enterprise soon flourished as norms of American life. For reasons which I shall discuss, Albany lagged behind in the fulfillment of these Revolutionary ideals. As Henry Christman has affirmed in his *Tin Horns and Calico,* early nineteenth-century Albany "was the seat of power of a landed aristocracy, the center of an island of semi-feudalism in a nation that had, little more than half a century before, declared the common faith in democracy and free enterprise." The Albany of the 1820s was thus far more agrarian and far less democratic than might be expected. The reader, then, should be prepared for a society conscious of maintaining its social distinctions, a society clinging to traditions inherited from Europe, rather than welcoming the rising tide of Jacksonian democracy.

A quick review of Albany's society and economy in the 1820s will help to remind us how conservative the city was. A convenient way of seeing the scope of the city's society is to return to 1788 and review a procession that marched through its streets to celebrate the adoption of the Federal Constitution.

Albany—though not its environs—had strongly favored the Constitution and the procession represented nearly every corporation or professional group in the city, a microcosm of Albany's society. Each professional group had its own banner, coat of arms, and motto, much as medieval English and Dutch guilds had done. Repre-

16

sented were Albany's trades: farmers, brewers, carpenters, gold and silver smiths, boatbuilders, tinmen and pewterers, block and pump makers, sailmakers, blacksmiths, clock and watch makers, barbers, bakers, nailers, clothiers, cartmen, millers and weavers, printers and glaziers, tailors, coachmakers and wheelwrights, turners, masons and bricklayers, saddlers and harnessmakers, tanners and curriers, brass founders, coopers, butchers, cordwainers, glassmakers. Their flags' mottos ranged from the piety of the saddlers and harnessmakers' "Our Trust is in God" to the butchers' vulgar "May we never want fat cattle." Certain trades had fitted out wagons with workshops on them: the blacksmiths' wagon, for instance, contained a forge and bellows with craftsmen at work. Besides the trades, present were representatives of the Albany Light Horse, the officers of the militia, the corporations of the Dutch, Episcopal, and Presbyterian churches, judges and lawyers, and schoolmasters and students. Here in visual terms was Albany's social and economic life.

What made this array especially representative of the upper Hudson Valley was the pre-eminence of agricultural symbols and the presence of heads of landed families, signifying Albany's dependence upon its hinterland. The parade opened with axmen from the timber trade, followed by an elegant plow, sowers, a neat harrow, and farmers with a flag emblazoned with a sheaf of wheat and their motto, "God speed the plow." Proof that the fortunes of the leading families were founded upon the agrarian interest was evident by their presence astride farm implements. These included John Cuyler, Jacob Lansing, and the Patroon himself, Stephen Van Rensselaer, the epitome of the landed aristocrat. As if his role in extracting the bounty of the land were not clear enough, a young Van Rensselaer followed on the brewers' dray, with a silver beaker in hand, dressed as the god Bacchus. The domination of the scene by the symbol of the wheat sheaf is verified by the fact that even the merchants used it on their flag. Later, when it came to selecting a coat of arms for the city, the wheat sheaf and the farmer were placed upon it, equal in importance to Albany's historic fur or Indian trade.

In the almost forty years that passed between the celebration of the Constitution and the events of Dr Jones' story, Albany grew and prospered, but the underpinning of its society remained constant. There was one jolt to its stability in 1797 when the city became the capital of the Empire State and hence a sort of court for politicians, lawyers, soldiers, and parasites. There was a second jolt in 1825 when the Erie Canal was completed, renewing the city's position as a terminus for westward settlement and trade. But the great families like the Van Rensselaers, Lansings, Cuylers, Schuylers, and Ten Broecks welcomed such opportunities, absorbed new blood into their ranks, and continued to dominate the city and countryside.

Writing of Albany in 1823, a traveler remarked that while the city showed signs of stirring industrialization and enterprise, "in proportion to its wealth and population," it "is not conspicuous in the extent of its manufactures." Albany held the industrial revolution at arm's length and paid the penalty by its lagging growth. In 1790, after 170 years of existence, the city had only a little more than 3,000 inhabitants—placing it well out of the top ten cities in the new republic. Though it was at that time the second largest city in the state, over the next half century it fell to third and then fourth place, behind Brooklyn and Buffalo, while Rochester and nearby Troy grew faster and closed the gap.

Lafayette visited the upper Hudson in 1824 and was impressed by Albany's rival, Troy, a city that had "arisen as if by enchantment" on a spot that during the Revolution was occupied by only a few cabins. Troy's rise—as well as that of Cohoes and Watervliet on the west side of the Hudson—provided a challenge for Albany from an industrialized society. Troy was founded after the Revolution by New Englanders who utilized abundant sources of water power to run machines at which skilled and unskilled labor turned out cut nails and sheet iron. While Albany had its share of entrepreneurs with factory interests, they eventually seem to have gravitated to Troy. Ironically, Erastus Corning's Albany Iron Works —where plates were made for the Monitor—was located in Troy and was ultimately absorbed by that city's famous Burden Iron Works.

Albany's economy was based upon a different system that dated back to the seventeenth century. The fur trade, then the Indian trade, and then the victualing of the armies had created a merchant community that by the mid-eighteenth century was secure in its position. While profits were made in each of these enterprises, none provided a lasting basis for the economy until the wheat and flour trade developed in the early eighteenth century. This business depended upon the ability of the Albany aristocracy to gather wheat from the hinterland, to process it into flour and ship it down the

1. View of Albany in the 1820s

North Pearl and State Streets, Albany, from Jacques Gérard Milbert's *Picturesque Itinerary of the Hudson River,* 1828-29. Courtesy: New York State Library.

Hudson to be sold in New York City, and then to return with cargoes of manufactured goods to be sold in area stores.

Philip Van Rensselaer, the Revolutionary War veteran who erected Cherry Hill in 1787, was heavily involved in this trade. He gathered wheat over the winter from tenant farmers who brought it by sled to his Albany warehouse; he then held it until prices were at their highest in New York City—braving the icy waters of the Hudson in his sloop, daring to be the first to go or the last to return with a cargo. On return trips the Van Rensselaer sloop was filled with linens, china, tea, buttons, pins, ribbons, lace, and silk—perhaps some of the very items that can be seen at Cherry Hill today.

The wheat trade was thus based in the countryside: wherever there were rich, flat lands for farming, or sources of waterpower for gristmills, or country stores for merchandising, or dock facilities for landings. Philip Van Rensselaer made his headquarters outside of Albany at Cherry Hill, while another of these rural entrepreneurs, his brother-in-law William Ludlow, chose Claverack. Ludlow was of an important New York City merchant family, but he selected Claverack for the seat of his enterprises because he knew the greatest profits were to be made in the countryside. The rents he collected from John Van Rensselaer's tenants came largely in the form of wheat and flour. This produce was shipped to his family firm in New York City in his brother-in-law's sloop and on the return trip the sloop brought goods to stock Ludlow's Claverack store. He prospered and in the same year that Cherry Hill was erected he built an elegant brick Georgian house to serve as the center of his Claverack business empire. Ludlow's home, Van Rensselaer's Cherry Hill, and other similar estates were working farms and seats of enterprise, not the pleasure palaces that country homes were in suburban Philadelphia. This dispersion of wealth and business meant that Albany was unable to clearly establish itself as the dominant economic center of the region—that is, unless it took into account these powerful agrarian interests.

These powerful interests did not remain at the top merely by virtue of their great houses and ties of kinship. The Albany aristocracy had to work and prove themselves to gain the acceptance of their peers, their tenants, and the city's populace. Philip Van Rensselaer's son, Philip P.—a character in the story—was a merchant like his father, but he was not as successful financially, for we know he was sued in 1818 for mismanaging Elsie Whipple's inheritance. His financial failure carried over to the public realm, where he lacked a military career and did not receive an office in local government. Aristocrats who failed to be enterprising and enlightened did not gain the respect of their peers and were cut off from the rewards of political office or social distinction.

Among the good works that gained respect for the aristocracy was their ability to develop Albany's hinterland, risking capital in order to prepare land for settlement, pushing back the boundaries of the frontier to the north and west. As early as the 1720s Johannes Schuyler developed his share of the Saratoga patent where the Fishkill Creek met the Hudson. The creek was the outlet for Saratoga Lake and along it he built a gristmill and a sawmill in addition to clearing land and erecting a fortified house. The exposed settlement was destroyed in 1745 and in 1777 as a result of the fortunes of war, but in each case it was rebuilt. In 1783 it was the scene of one of the most important social events of the era, the marriage between Stephen Van Rensselaer and Philip Schuyler's daughter Margaret — a sign of commitment to the settlement by the two most powerful families in the region.

Nor were the Schuylers alone: Peter Gansevoort, the hero of Fort Stanwix, put up a gristmill, two sawmills, and a general store at his Snock Kill farm, only a few miles to the north of the Schuyler patent. In another instance of Albany enterprise, the Caldwells, James and William, father and son, built a community at the head of Lake George, operating a gristmill, an iron forge, and steamboats and logging rafts from the landing that was eventually to become Lake George Village. Investments such as these were risky and rarely more than moderately profitable; yet the Albany aristocracy involved itself in such developments, motivated as much by a concern to have a legacy as a desire for wealth.

To their credit the aristocracy were also committed to the rational, scientific, and practical aspects of learning, which we call the Enlightenment. Enlightened thinkers believed that society could be improved through the application of technology. Practical and technical education was necessary to produce the conditions to foster expansion and improvement.

These attitudes did not foster the development of Albany as a great educational center. In 1795 Albany lost out to Schenectady in the race to establish a school of higher learning which ultimately became Union College. Even Albany's great benefactor, Stephen Van Rensselaer, ignored the city in 1824 choosing industrial Troy as the site for the Rensselaer School, an institution for the application of science to everyday life that was to become Rensselaer Polytechnic Institute.

Part of the Albany aristocracy's failure to obtain a college may be attributed to their reluctance to put a high premium on a college education. They viewed such institutions as a civic ornament, not necessarily a place where they would educate their children. Among Cherry Hill's first two generations of Van Rensselaers, while most had some schooling, only one of the sixteen who grew to maturity graduated from a college (Union in 1812). Their view of education was more practical, emphasizing the acquisition of skills so that one could succeed in the countinghouse, at running a household or in managing a farm.

Of far greater concern to them than the education of children was the education of farmers. Founded and chartered from 1791 to 1793, the Society for the Promotion of Agriculture, Arts and Manufactures served as a forum for landowners to present scientific solutions to pressing agricultural problems. Albanians like Stephen Van Rensselaer, John Lansing Jr., and Simon De Witt led the Society, which finally chose Albany as its home in 1800. Four years later it was rechristened the Society for the Promotion of Useful Arts, a misleading title, in that ninety percent of the papers involved agricultural topics. A sampling of the proceedings reveals articles on drilling procedures to plant wheat, on the use of seaweed for fodder, and on controlling the devastating effect of the Hessian fly. Also found in its pages is a respect for English agriculture, the pace setter in terms of scientific innovation, and happily—for the Patroon at least—an agriculture which still gave the landlord the leading role in creating productive acreage.

One result of these activities was the publication of handbooks for the average farmer, that would provide him with the techniques of scientific agriculture, ensuring that New York State would remain "the granary of the world." Such a book was John Nicholson's *The Farmer's Assistant,* published in 1814, which claimed that the reader could "become as fully enlightened as possible in all that tends to render his labors productive." The book was used by farmers great and small. Solomon Van Rensselaer had a copy to aid him and his wife Arriet in running Mount Hope and later Cherry Hill farm. This volume represented the type of practical education that the aristocracy appreciated—one that had the goal of furthering the agrarian basis of the economy and society.

Enlightened as they were, the aristocracy could never have remained on top without a certain acquiescence from the middle and lower classes. In 1827, when 30,000 people gathered to see what proved to be the last public hanging in Albany, there were shudders from the well-bred who saw this throng as a potential threat to social convention. The mere fact that women viewed the hanging was considered revolutionary. Yet the crowd was far from being revolutionary; in fact the bulk of them shared the same conservative attitudes as their betters. Let us look at the spectators.

The majority of the throng was made up of farmers who had traveled from as far away as Cooperstown, causing the crush of carriages and wagons described by Dr. Jones. These farmers can be divided into three groups: the freeholders who owned their land, the tenants who rented it, the farm laborers who worked for wages as hired hands. The accused murderer belonged to the third category. The hanging took place a decade before the death of the Patroon, Stephen Van Rensselaer, a decade before the Anti-Rent Wars which rocked his lands. It is accepted that he was a lenient landlord, who rarely extracted rents to the fullest and a man who treated his tenants humanely, so that his lands had become heavily populated with lease-holding New Englanders. More work needs to be done on the state of the Patroon's lands at the time of the murder before conclusions are made, but such an analysis would have to struggle with the fact that some tenants placed the Patroon's good will above their desire to own land.

As to Albany's population of about 15,000 shopkeepers, mechanics, and laborers our knowledge is also limited. Documents of the 1820s show that there were three broad occupational groups in the city: the builders, the food processors, those involved in providing transportation and lodging. Within the first group were lumber dealers, carpenters, and stonemasons; within the second were grocers, victualers, confectioners, and brewers; within the third were teamsters, coachmen and coachmakers, blacksmiths, harness and tram makers, boatmen, skippers, ship captains, sailmakers, stevedores and cartmen, innkeepers and hotel owners. Since the 1788 procession there had been a rise in the economy's transportation sector, but on the whole the means of making a living had not changed.

Nor had the attitude of these men and women toward their betters: it was the goal of the shopkeepers to become landed aristocrats and the goal of the craftsmen to become shopkeepers. Many belonged to the Albany Republican Artillery, a unit of citizen-soldiers founded in 1809, that held balls, entertained on steamboat excursions, and escorted dignitaries to the theater—all occasions in which to show off their uniforms. Their respect for order and property is seen in the 1840s when they were one of the chief arms of the law in putting down the Anti-Rent Wars. Albany's craftsmen and shopkeepers were too involved in their Masonic lodges, their banks, and their businesses to have sympathy for the conditions of the Van Rensselaer tenants.

Blacks were also present in the crowd on hanging day, some of them having been freed only a few weeks before on July 4. This act was the culmination of a legislative program of manumission that had begun in 1799 and was expanded in 1817. It is important to review where Albany County stood on this issue. In the eighteenth century, New York's dependence upon slavery was greater than any place north of Maryland and Albany County was one of the chief slaveholding regions of both the colony and the state. The Census of 1790 shows that there were more slaves in the county than any other part of the state, not only because there were more blacks, but also because of the slow spread of voluntary manumission. While only four percent of Albany County's blacks had been freed, the state-wide average was eighteen percent and in populous New York City it was thirty-one percent. In the decades that followed the number of slaves declined rapidly—much more quickly than in Ulster or Orange Counties—yet in 1820 there were still well over 1,000 slaves in Albany and Columbia Counties. What reluctance there was for manumission was not racial—most landlords who supported the Revolution believed in the universal rights of man—rather it was economic since such action violated the rights of property. Besides, the observations of Anne Grant, first published in 1808, claimed that masters regarded their slaves as far better workers than the growing influx of New Englanders. Such respect must have mitigated friction between slaves and their masters.

Respect for the leadership provided by the Albany aristocracy kept farmers, craftsmen, shopkeepers, laborers and blacks content—at least until the Anti-Rent Wars of the 1840s. This aristocracy built its wealth on exploitation of the land, whether in renting, milling, food processing, lumbering, or merchandising. In the ways of commercial enterprise and their enlightened attitude toward technology they were in the forefront of the age, but when it came to dealing with the populace they demanded respect and felt no need to test every case at the ballot box with universal male suffrage. Such leaders made Albany a conservative place, a community where social distinction contributed to the stability of society.

What the reader now has is an understanding of the times which he or she may use to comprehend the Strang-Whipple Case. There is also a built-in warning that the reader should not be too doctrinaire in applying this knowledge. It is accepted, for instance, that in affairs of the heart, social barriers will fall. Indeed they do in this book for the story's crucial love affair involves a member of the aristocracy and a mere hired hand. The pages that follow will show us an Albany society that largely conforms to the above description — but there are always exceptions, always the moment of passion when traditions are broken. Here is a slice of social history that the reader will both enjoy and contemplate.

Murder at Cherry Hill

CHAPTER 1

Dramatis Personae

In 1826 Albany was better than two hundred years old, but suddenly its economic blood was quickening. The impact of the year-old Erie Canal was felt on all sides; thousands of families headed for the west funneled through the narrow streets; already, too, the produce of the west was being transferred to increasing numbers of fast steamboats plying between Albany and New York. Back of the bustling docks, back of the banks, the hotels and taverns there were families that had controlled Albany since the days of the fur trade—Schuylers, Lansings, Knickerbackers, and greatest of all, the Van Rensselaers. In taste, social position, economic power this was the in-group, close knit, conservative, shrewd, powerful.

This is the story of a scandal that shook that eminently respectable world to its foundations, a tale of passion in a family where all emotion was kept under firm control, of notoriety where privacy was valued at the highest price, of murder in the dark of night, of a hanging that drew an audience of thirty thousand.

Cherry Hill, the mansion where much of the action took place, still stands, no longer surrounded by orchards and farm lands but still sitting on its sharply rising hillside, looking down on South Pearl Street, its once magnificent view of the Hudson River interrupted now by superhighways and industrial growth. It is just at the edge of the city and was one of the first farms south of the city line. Not only does Cherry Hill still stand, but many of the furnishings which were there in 1826-27 are still there and the mansion is open to the public as a historic house. Visitors who know eighteenth- and nineteenth-century American furniture are fascinated as they go through the rooms; students of architecture find the place a delight.

The present residence of Cherry Hill was completed in 1787 for Philip Van Rensselaer and Maria Sanders, his wife, replacing the residence they had occupied since their marriage in 1768. He was a merchant, farmer and tanner, a cousin of the Patroon and during the Revolution a Commissary of Military Stores for the Northern Department, gathering supplies for the Continental Army. Philip was a shrewd businessman and could well afford the new house he had built for the family he and Maria were raising; of their thirteen children, nine grew to adulthood. Philip Van Rensselaer plays no direct part in this story, for he died in 1798, but one inevitably comes to feel that Maria, "the old lady" by 1827, was a force of nature. We seldom see her close to, but back in the shadows of the northeast bedroom, there she is, listening, knowing, disapproving.

Maria had the right of occupancy of the whole north side of the house as long as she lived; her son Philip P. Van Rensselaer and his family occupied the south side. As in most of the great houses of its time, a wide hall ran from front to back on the first and second floors; this presumably was common to both families but the old lady's side of the house was separate and distinct and not entered casually. At her disposal was the gracious parlor on the first floor with a smaller room behind it—perhaps then, as now, an office. Between the office and the great hall, where a washroom now is, was originally an enclosed stairway which went from cellar to attic, primarily for servants, but it provided an inconspicuous pathway for the family. On the second floor, up the main stairway, Maria enjoyed the spacious master bedroom, looking east toward the river, a room enhanced by a fireplace and containing furniture she inherited from her father, the merchant Robert Sanders. Behind her room and next to the stairs was another bedroom, presumably that of her daughter, Maria Matilda. Somewhere in that side of the house lived her son Kilian, perhaps on the third floor where there were several rooms which both families seem to have used, even as both families used the inner stairway mentioned above. The fourth person in the old lady's household was a ten-year-old white serving girl.

It was somewhat more crowded on the south side of the house. The head of the household was Philip P. Van Rensselaer, son of Philip and Maria, forty-three years old and presumably in vigorous health in 1826;

2. Ground Plan of Cherry Hill, 1826-27

Cherry Hill faces the Hudson River toward the east. The city of Albany is to the north, where the Bethlehem Turnpike becomes South Pearl Street. For a bird's-eye view, see Illustration 7 on page 83.

Hudson River

Island Creek

Meadow

←Albany Bethlehem Turnpike (South Pearl St.)

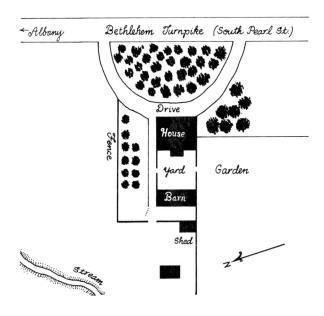

Drive

Fence

House

Yard

Barn

Garden

Shed

stream

37

he was to die mysteriously early the next year—mysteriously, but I believe quite naturally. Unlike his father, Philip P. had not prospered and by the time of his death he was very close to bankruptcy. This may account in part for the family's willingness to take in the Whipples as paying guests. Philip P.'s wife, Catharine, was the daughter of old Abraham A. Lansing, a successful river captain and for some years Philip P.'s business partner; Lansings and Van Rensselaers had intermarried frequently, and Catharine's mother was a daughter of Kilian Van Rensselaer. Old Captain Lansing had died at Cherry Hill in 1822.

Philip and Catharine had seven children, four of whom were alive and living in the house, Abraham, aged 21, Maria, 18, Elsie, 10, and little Arriete, 8. The father and mother presumably occupied the front bedroom on the south side, with the children on the third floor. The southwest bedroom was rented out to a couple named John and Elsie Whipple, a pleasant room with a fireplace, one section of the room partially partitioned off for a bed. The west window looked out on the roof of a shed that then ran twenty feet along the back of the house. Elsie Whipple was Catharine Van Rensselaer's niece, the daughter of her deceased brother, Abraham D. Lansing. The Whipples had a boy, Abraham, five years old in 1826. John Whipple's niece also lived there when John was away; Henrietta Patrick slept with Elsie on those occasions.

The servants slept in the cellar and since much of the action of this story takes place there, we would do well to look at it carefully. Remember that this house is set into a hillside, facing east; while the cellar is below ground on the west, it is fully exposed in the front. There are doors at both the north and south sides and there was probably one in the center of the east side, beneath the high stoop that led to the first floor entry.

There were two kitchens, one on either side of the house. There is no evidence what the north side was used for in the 1820s; certainly all the cooking was done in the room in the southeast corner. This was presided over by Dinah Jackson, fifty years old, a black slave who must have been looking forward to July 4, 1827, when slavery would end in New York State. Dinah was nobody's fool, a woman of character, shrewdness and warmth. Her bedroom was one of the two behind the kitchen; there were two others off the north kitchen. In the room next to Dinah's slept two hired men; one was known as Joseph Orton and the other was George Wilson. On the north side slept George's brother, William Wilson, in one room and in the other a black boy who ran away that winter. Orton was called "Doctor" by the household because he wore glasses and could read and write some. His real name was Jesse Strang and Strang is the name by which we shall refer to him.

The time has come to separate from this crowd of seventeen or eighteen people, living under that one roof, the three principals of my story. We start with Elsie Whipple.

Elsie Lansing Whipple was complex as the neurotic always seem to be complex. She was the daughter and granddaughter of hysterical, undisciplined women who pampered her and brought her up without any usable moral code. Her grandfather, Capt. Abraham A. Lansing, the river boat captain, amassed a sizable fortune which

3. *Inside Cherry Hill*

Key

1. Maria Matilda Van Rensselaer's room
2. Hall
3. The Whipples' room
4. Office
5. Enclosed stairway
6. Shed
7. After Philip P. Van Rensselaer's death, his wife Catharine Van Rensselaer's room
8. Black boy's room
9. William Wilson's room
10. Dinah Jackson's room
11. George Wilson and Jesse Strang's room
12. Maria Sanders Van Rensselaer's room
13. Philip P. and Catharine Van Rensselaer's room until Philip P.'s death; then their son Abraham Van Rensselaer's room
14. North parlor
15. South parlor

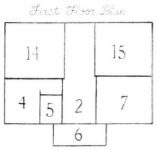

First Floor Plan

Second Floor Plan

41

he divided among his children while still alive. He was especially generous to his only son, Elsie's father, Abraham D. Lansing, who died when Elsie was a small child.

Elsie wouldn't study and her grandfather was afraid that as long as she was under the indulgent influence of her mother she would never amount to anything and would grow up an ignoramus. There were family scenes but finally the old man had his way; Elsie went off to a female seminary in Troy, the only concession being that her mother was permitted to see her every Saturday. This arrangement lasted for three months, when suddenly her mother died and Elsie became the responsibility of her aunts. This would be sometime around 1816 when Elsie was fourteen, and a very difficult, unmanageable fourteen at that, too pretty for her own good, physically more mature than her years, indifferent to truth or falsehood, and full of animal spirits.

The girl was transferred to a school in Waterford and stayed there a full quarter, at the end of which her grandfather came for her so that she might spend her two weeks vacation at home. Next door to the Lansings lived another successful river boat family consisting of Captain Barnum Whipple and his wife, who was a relation of the Lansings, their children, and the Captain's brother John, now twenty-four years old. It would appear that whatever may have been the ties of common occupation and kinship, the Lansings and Whipples were not on very good terms.

Every evening after supper little Elsie skipped out of the house and came skipping back just in time for family prayers at ten o'clock. When they asked her where she had been, she told them that she had been visiting the B's, a family that lived on the far side of the Whipples. When vacation came to an end, she went back to Waterford for another quarter of schooling, at the end of which her grandfather came for her. The term ended on Friday; using all her wiles, all her pretty ways, she persuaded him she couldn't go that day, nor Sunday, nor Monday. Tuesday morning she had disappeared. The family were alarmed and puzzled, for as Elsie's aunt said to Mrs. B., all during her vacation Elsie had visited no house but the B's. But Mrs. B. knew better; Elsie would come directly to the B's after her supper, stay but a few moments, and then slip into the Whipples' house, where she and John Whipple had plenty of opportunity to get acquainted. Soon word came that she and John were married. One can safely wager that the scheme for elopement was Elsie's; it has her trade-mark on it. Her grandfather was furious.

Captain Lansing tried to regain from Elsie the real estate and money which he had earlier given her father. To the Lansings, John Whipple may well have seemed an impoverished fortune hunter, for as his brother's assistant he probably earned very little. And here was pretty, fourteen-year-old Elsie with all that money being trapped into matrimony by a young man nine years her senior. And when John Whipple took his demand for his wife's real estate to the Court of Chancery and won, the old Captain had had his bellyful and died before there was any reconciliation. His co-defendant, Philip P. Van Rensselaer, the Captain's son-in-law and Elsie's guardian and uncle by marriage, came in time to feel differently about Whipple.

The

Van Rensselaer

Maria Sanders ¹⁷⁶⁸— Philip Van Rensselaer
1749 - 1830   1747 - 1798

Kilian   Maria   Philip P. Van Rensselaer
1780-1829   Matilda   1783-1827
               1787-1856

Abraham   Maria P.   Elsie   Arriete
b. 1805   b. 1808   b.1816   b.1818

Albany's leading families intermarried and cemented *
relationships with business partnerships. Philip P. Van
Rensselaer was the first cousin of his bride Catharine
Lansing. He was also the merchant partner of his unc
and father-in-law, Abraham A. Lansing, river captain

nilies

Lansing

sie Schuyler
in Rensselaer
d. 1796
= Abraham A. Lansing
1752 - 1822

tharine Lansing)
1783 - 1867

Abraham
D. Lansing)
1775 - 1805
= Christina
Voorhees

John Whipple
1792 - 1827
he murder victim)
c. 1817 Elsie Lansing)
1802 - 1832

Abraham D. L. Whipple
1821 - 1890

RON TOELKE

45

John Whipple was of the breed of decent fellows who have all the right virtues for their time and place. By 1826, at thirty-four he was already a success in a rapidly expanding economy. His people were New Englanders, his father having served in the Connecticut line during the Revolution, after which he moved into western Massachusetts, thence to southern Vermont where he still operated the family farm. John's brother, Barnum, was captain of a Hudson River sloop, running between Albany and New York. In 1811, when John was eighteen, he came to Albany and was apprenticed to Barnum to learn river navigation; at his brother's expense he also studied accounting and penmanship. For a while John served as Barnum's second in command and presumably this was how he was employed when he came to know Elsie Lansing.

It was characteristic of John Whipple that he took his wife's inheritance, nourished it, invested it wisely and made of it far more than it had been. He obtained command of a river sloop and pursued his calling "with the industry, skillfulness, fidelity and perseverance for which he was afterward remarkable." In the mid-1820s he had become a contractor, working on the Delaware and Hudson Canal which was to connect the coal fields of Pennsylvania with Kingston and the Hudson Valley markets.

John Whipple was not reconciled to Elsie's grandfather before the old Captain died but sometime after he had won his case in the Court of Chancery, the rest of her family recognized that here was an honest, earnest fellow who had not married their kinswoman for her money. It may be that they were also aware that whatever Elsie's attraction to John may have been, he was paying a heavy price for it. He was patient beyond measure—patient with her frivolity, her self-pity, her tears, her hysterics, with her inability to come to grips with reality. He was protective and kind, but this was no partnership built upon respect and confidence.

The move to Cherry Hill was typical of his protectiveness. There Elsie would be surrounded by her kinsfolk, she would not be so lonesome while he was back and forth to his work on the Canal. She was a beautiful woman with long golden hair but so lacking in good horse sense that she needed to be among older and wiser heads than hers. There may have been another factor: this was not a wife about whom a man could be confident and in the midst of a large watchful household she would be less likely to stray. If this was his thinking, he overestimated their watchfulness.

In the balanced, classical prose of its time the *Albany Argus and City Gazette* (Aug. 11, 1827) summarized Whipple's character as

dutiful and generous as a son; grateful and kind as a brother; faithful as a friend; affectionate as a father; and as a husband constant, tender, considerate and confiding. As a member of society, he was already distinguished for his usefulness; as a man of business he was prudent, attentive, persevering; economical and temperate in his habits, and strictly just in his dealings. As a man he was mild and cheerful in his temper, conciliatory and respectful in his deportment, frank in disposition and manners, prepossessing in appearance and address. And above all, sensible of his

47

obligations to his Maker for the blessings conferred on him, for the prosperity and reputation he enjoyed and for all the mercies of his existence.

If one were to select carefully a list of adjectives, the very opposite of those chosen by the *Argus* to describe John Whipple, he would come close to characterizing Jesse Strang, alias Joseph Orton. About all they had in common was their backgrounds. Daniel Strang, Jesse's father, was a hardworking, decent farmer in Dutchess County; he and his first wife had seven children, of whom Jesse was the eldest; Daniel's second wife, by 1827, was the mother of seven more. Jesse was born in 1797 in Yorktown, Westchester County; at the age of eighteen he married Deborah H. Lounsberry of Fishkill. Four children were born to that marriage before 1825, when Jesse deserted his family and went to Sandusky, Ohio. In the spring of 1826 he returned east. Somewhere in western New York he perpetrated a hoax to leave the impression that he had been murdered. He left by a lakeside torn clothes, ripped saddlebags and an area scuffed and trampled to look as though a struggle had taken place. Later the lake was dragged and word went out that Jesse Strang was dead and his body lost. The man who had walked away from that place was now called Joseph Orton.

He was a short, stocky man, swarthy with black eyes and a head of black bushy hair, cut short. He could read and write and wore glasses, giving him a studious appearance unusual among workingmen; this is why the household called him "Doctor." He was a good worker when he wished and in less than a year's time, while employed by the Van Rensselaers, he increased his wages by fifty percent, starting at ten dollars a month and ending at fifteen dollars a month. He was a general farmhand; we get glimpses of him threshing, cutting, hauling and selling wood, picking nuts, taking care of the horses; he could fix a lock or replace a broken window. He was agreeable enough and John Whipple, at least, seems to have liked him. But he lived part of his life in a dream world. The bizarre plots, the dreams of money coming from non-existent debtors, the hoax by which he rid the world of Jesse Strang and created Joseph Orton are part of his incapacity for dealing with life as it is. Add to these qualities his garrulousness and his lack of good common sense.

Strang had come to Albany through a series of accidents. He had been headed for Stillwater, where he had relatives, but from Schenectady his trunk was sent by error to Albany, thence to New York by steamboat. The wrong trunk came back and there was more waiting. One day he went to Greenbush (now Rensselaer) where he ran into an Albany tavern keeper named Otis Bates who hired him and he went to work for Bates the 15th of July, 1826.

Strang had been working for Bates about three weeks when one evening, toward sunset, he walked into the barroom to find two girls there. One of them he may have recognized as Maria Van Rensselaer, the daughter of Philip P. Van Rensselaer, Bates' landlord and the owner of Cherry Hill, sixty rods north of Bates' tavern on what is now South Pearl Street. But it was the other girl who caught his eye. She was "sprightly, playful and giddy" and she was pushing Mr. Bates around his barroom in a most unladylike fashion. That night, in bed with Bates' son, Otis Jr., Strang asked him who she might be, adding, "I should like to sleep with her." It was Strang's recollection—although young Bates denied it later on—that he replied, "How do you know but you can, until after you have tried, for I have." The "sprightly girl" was Mrs. John Whipple. A few days later, while Strang was in Bates' barn threshing, Elsie and the Bates girl came and watched him work, but no words passed between them. She was just looking.

On August 28, 1826, Jesse Strang hired out to Philip P. Van Rensselaer, Esq., for ten dollars a month, room and board thrown in; he moved to Cherry Hill, into the bedroom next to Dinah Jackson.

The day after Jesse Strang went to work at Cherry Hill, John Whipple and his wife Elsie went to Kingston where he had contracts to build part of the Delaware and Hudson Canal. Others had predicted this would ruin him but actually he cleared $4,000, probably the equivalent of $60,000 today. They were gone for a month during which time Strang was becoming an accepted member of the household. Late in September the Whipples returned, but about October 1 John went back to Kingston alone. Life flowed on in the big house, the black boy Jack absconded, Henrietta Patrick, John Whipple's niece, a tailoress by trade, came to stay with Elsie, sleeping in her room with her, going back and forth the mile to town to her work.

From the first day he had seen her wrestling in Bates' tavern bar, Strang had felt an increasing "sensation of amorous desire" for Elsie Whipple but there were no signals from her. On the 20th of October a group of them went out gathering nuts: Philip P. Van Rensselaer, the master of the house, his son Abraham, his daughter Maria, Elsie Whipple, Henrietta Patrick and Strang. That evening, in the kitchen, Elsie started up a conversation with him about the conduct and appearance that day of Maria and Henrietta. In commenting on her peers to a hired man, Elsie made the first move in breaking the class barriers between them and he was quick to interpret it as a sign that she liked him.

A day or so later, after finishing his dinner, he went out in front of the house, a few feet from the stoop. Leaning against the post of the stoop was Elsie. "Doctor," she said, "I want you to write me a letter." His first assumption was that she was illiterate and wanted him to write a letter for her, but on second thought he wasn't so sure.

"What, I write *you* a letter?"

"Yes," answered the voice of experience, "I hate to write the first one. I want you to consider well of it from this to the bush [the woods], and back again; and I want you to write tonight."

He left her and went off with his team to cut and haul wood, thinking about her request. Was it a trap to expose him to her husband? But then he thought about what young Bates had told him that night as they lay in bed. He thought of the time she had come to watch him threshing in the barn and of what she had said to him in the kitchen after they had been picking nuts. He thought about how much he wanted her and he decided to write the letter, come what might. The next morning, sitting in the big south kitchen, he wrote her the first of the long series of letters that was to pass between them. Probably seldom have there been two people living in the same household and in daily contact who have been such constant (and such foolish) correspondents.

Dear Elsie [he remembered writing her], I have seariesly considred on it as you requested of me yeasterday and I have concluded two compose a few lines two You and I thought that it was not my duty two right very freely not nowing Your object perhaps it is two get sum of my righting two show two your husband as you ar a marid woman, and If that is your intenslıln It is my whish fore you two let me now it fore it is a thing that I skorn two make a distirbance between you and your husband but If on the outher hand It is out of pure offections I should be quite hapy for two have the information in your hand riting and I hope that you will not take any offen [offense] in my maner of riting two you as we ar pirfict strangers two each other, but hop that thoes few lines may find free exceptan with you and after I find out your motive I can right mour freely on the subject and as for my offections thay are quite favorable I shall expact an answer from you If that is your motive, sow I remain your well whisher, JOSEPH ORTON.

This is the letter as he reconstructed it ten months later. He remembered that Sunday morning when he wrote it and how she was standing by the stove in the kitchen when he handed it to her. Half an hour later, again in the kitchen, she put her answer in his hands and it read something like this:

Dear Doctor—

It is true I am a married woman, and we are entire strangers to each other; I had no evil design on you in requesting you to write to me. My motive is from pure love for you, excited when I first saw you. The first time I ever saw you, to be acquainted with you, I fell in love with your eyes; nor have I, while you are absent, any comfort or happiness while thinking of you. And if I am a married woman, I ran away to get married, and I can do so again. For some time past I have wanted to express my affection for you, but have been waiting in the hopes that you would broach the subject, and this was the reason of my asking you to write me a letter, hoping that you would express your feelings towards me; and if your affections for me are as great as mine for you, you will never leave here without taking me with you. I hope you will write to me immediately, and let me know whether you have any affection for me. I have often expressed my opinion, that there was no such thing as love; but I have now altered my opinion, and am satisfied of its influence, and that you are the only one I ever did love.

I remain your true and affectionate lover until death separates us.

Elsie D. Whipple

She superscribed it "To Mr. John Whipple, Kingston, Ulster County" lest someone pick it up, but she did not seal it. "Doctor" no sooner received it than he sat down in the kitchen, surrounded by the family, and wrote her a reply, superscribing it "To Mr. E. Huested, Lower

Sandusky, Sandusky County, State of Ohio." Between two and three o'clock that afternoon he gave her this, still in the kitchen, unnoticed by any of the family. Before dark she had her reply in his hands. The gist of this correspondence and that which followed was that each was in love with the other and Elsie was ready to fly anywhere he said, so long as she had $1,200 to take with them. To a man earning 33¢ a day this was the rough equivalent of $15,000 today.

In any event, thus began the shuttling back and forth of a correspondence which has the theatrical qualities of a Shakespearean play and the psychological implica tions of a guilty couple who were subconsciously wanting to be caught. As months went by, they used other members of the household as letter carriers; sometimes they secreted their missives for the other to pick up. In one respect they were careful, they seem always to have burned the letters after reading. Those I have quoted are as Strang remembered them months later. Up to a certain point one sees them as part of a shared fantasy, but when Elsie gets down to cases and puts her finger on $1,200 as the necessary price of elopement we are on the bedrock of reality.

That same Sunday evening, October 22, 1826, they found themselves alone in the kitchen of that crowded household. Elsie said she had always wanted to keep a public house (actually she had inherited and was the owner of the Columbian Hotel in Albany) and if they could get $1,200 she thought she could furnish a public house well. Strang didn't know anything about keeping a public house but he thought he could turn his hand to that, as well as anything else. Later they considered heading for Montreal, until "Whipple should become reconciled in his mind," and then go on to Sandusky, Ohio, where Strang thought they could do a brisk business. They would be married under assumed names. These were their dream castles.

The irony which plagued Elsie Whipple, and perhaps Jesse Strang, too, was the simple fact the Elsie possessed several times $1,200 in her own name. But the laws of the time put her fortune entirely in the hands of her husband; she could leave him, she might just possibly divorce him or he, her, but the money remained in his hands. If Whipple were dead, and only then, could Elsie and "the Doctor" get their hands on her inheritance. Of course, if Whipple were dead, there would also be the money he had made by his own industry and acumen. It would take time and pressures not yet exerted to make Strang see that the key to the solution of all their problems lay in the words "if Whipple were dead," but by the 21st of November Elsie knew that there lay the solution.

CHAPTER 2

The Tryst

Two old-fashioned words inevitably come to mind as the tragedy we are considering unfolds: lust and avarice. There are other words—stupidity, hysteria, fantasy, fear—but one comes back to the strong physical attraction between Elsie Whipple and Jesse Strang which was, I think, perfectly mutual and was second only to their common interest in money, her money, Whipple's money, the imaginary money Strang pretended he had coming to him. They were psychological cripples, incapable of love but each was under the illusion that money could free them from the traps in which they felt themselves.

All through the winter and early spring of 1827 they made gestures toward the murder of John Whipple. It was begun with a letter from Elsie, written on 21 November 1826, according to Strang's *Confession*, in which she declared she wanted to lay a plan to take Whipple's life. Her suggestion was that Strang go to Kingston and hire himself out to Whipple's partner, a Mr. Stone, and then get some of the Irishmen working on the canal to do it or do the job himself. If he decided on the latter course, she would provide Strang with a brace of her husband's pistols.

Strang's first reaction to this approach was genuine fear; this was more than he had bargained for. By morning she had her reply; his feelings, he wrote, were impossible to g_t over: his affection for her was as great as any man's could be, but to take John Whipple's life, that he could not do. He loved her for herself, not her property, and before he would commit murder he would remain in his present position for the rest of his life. He would work himself to death for her before he would take her innocent husband's life. If this was the only way of obtaining her, then this was the end. At least this is what he said he thought he wrote to her, thinking about it nine months later. In a slightly more objective mood he thought his motives had been a genuine abhorrence to murder and a desire to find out whether she was really serious and to discover how firmly she would adhere to the proposal. There may have been more of the latter than the former.

In her reply Elsie tried a new tack. There was another man in her life, Mr. _____, and she had thought Strang as resolute as he. Mr. _____ was ready to take Whipple's life and he only wanted her property; he didn't really care for her, nor she for him. If Strang were as fond of her as he pretended, then he would do the deed and have both her and the property, to "live above board

57

and without work." But—one can almost hear a sad little sigh—since Strang had refused, she would endeavor to obtain the means to run away and leave Whipple. The trouble was that she couldn't bear the thought of leaving him with all her property to enjoy with another woman.

The weeks passed with no more specific suggestions of murder for a while. Elsie would say she wished John would die or get killed by laborers on the canal but none of the daily letters—sometimes delivered by eleven-year-old Elsie Van Rensselaer—were specific in their suggestions. John was at Cherry Hill most of January 1827 while work on the canal was impossible. One day Elsie came to Strang in the kitchen and tried again to arouse him to action.

One hears her complaining voice and senses the trembling intensity of her manner. "I have no other friend on earth but you. It's natural to run to you when I have any difficulty, John has struck me!" This was the hook to catch him on; he struck at her bait, then retreated but not for long.

"Shall I waylay him and kill him?"

"Yes."

"I can't."

"If you are so fainthearted, you must consent to get some poison and I'll do it myself. If you won't consent to get the poison, I will take my own life, for I won't take his abuse any longer."

Strang refused, but not for long. The urging went on for several days. One night she was on the way to her husband's room with a bowl of milk for him. To Strang she said, "If you had consented to get the poison, how easy it would be for me to just put it in and never be suspected."

About a week after the subject of poison first came up, Strang made a counterproposal in one of his letters. Instead of bringing poison into the house where there might be an accident, let Elsie get $300 and he would go to Montreal and hire a killer who would do the job. This threw the initiative back to Elsie and there were innumerable letters and conversations about ways and means.

On February 17 Philip P. Van Rensselaer died suddenly. The master of Cherry Hill left his wife Catharine Lansing and four children. Abraham, aged twenty-two, found himself the nominal head of a houseful of women —his grandmother, his mother, an aunt, three sisters, three female servants, Henrietta Patrick and, of course, Elsie Whipple. There were two or three hired men, one of whom was Strang. (Abraham had a shadowy uncle Kilian, aged forty-seven, who lived at Cherry Hill and who barely enters this story at all.)

Young Van Rensselaer did the sensible thing. He turned to John Whipple, a mature even-handed man of affairs, for counsel and advice. There was a very active farm to run and there was probably real estate to administer; no family with as many interests as the Van Rensselaers could avoid the changes the Erie Canal was bringing to Albany. John Whipple was a good man to listen to, but John was in Kingston and New York much of the time and Abraham was young and inexperienced. Life went on in Cherry Hill but there was no strong masculine hand on the tiller.

About the time Philip P. Van Rensselaer died, Elsie

came down with chicken pox and was in bed for about a week but by early March she was back in the kitchen where so much of the family life was carried on. While she was ill two women were brought in to care for her and presumably her little Abraham. They were enlisted to carry letters back and forth between Elsie and Strang, which were in due time burned or destroyed. One of these was Elsie's reply to his $300 suggestion: the only place she could raise the money was at the Columbian Hotel which she owned, but if she did, Philander Fobes, who managed it, would tell her husband. So it would have to be poison; Strang went up to South Pearl Street to the druggist opposite Crosby's hotel where he bought sixpence worth of arsenic, with the poisoner's usual explanation that it was "for rats." Next day he gave Elsie a spoonful of the white powder in paper and hid the rest in the loft of the barn where it blew to the floor and was found by Abraham Van Rensselaer who gave it to Whipple. When Whipple asked Dr. Wing what it was, he said he couldn't tell. Might be plaster of Paris. As it turned out, neither this nor any of the other parcels of arsenic Strang bought was ever analyzed.

On March 10 Elsie made the first attempt on John's life when, as Strang reported in his *Confession*, she came to him and said, "What have I done? I have given Mr. Whipple some poison in his tea. Aunt Caty [Mrs. Philip P. Van Rensselaer] is gone and I had a fine chance." A single small dose of arsenic is not very effective and Whipple made no complaint. In the meantime the two accomplices had pledged solemn oaths that if Whipple died neither would inform on the other and that if either were found out, the other would confess and they would be hanged together.

Since Elsie had thrown the remainder of her supply of arsenic in the fire lest she be discovered, Strang bought another sixpence worth from another druggist, folded a teaspoonful in each of three pieces of paper and hid the balance in a rafter of the barn. A week later she gave her husband a dose in his sulphur (presumably mixed with molasses, a standard spring tonic to "clean the blood"). She wondered if it would work in sulphur and Strang was sure it would circulate through the system. This brought on slightly better results: it "cramped his stomach" and she told Whipple it had done the same to her. Next morning she gave him some more sulphur—again with arsenic added. He took what he wanted and then gave little Abraham a spoonful and then made Elsie take the same. Unnoticed, she spit hers out but she was genuinely concerned for her son. At Strang's suggestion, she gave him some salt as a counter-agent. There is a suggestion of Elsie's ineptness as a housewife in the fact that with three or four barrels in the cellar, containing a variety of staples, she didn't know which was the salt barrel and Strang had to get a lump for her. Next morning both father and son were still in good health.

One day toward the end of March Dinah Jackson was preparing dinner and Strang was sitting idly in the kitchen. The tone and content of the beginning of the conversation are lost but finally he asked her if she would poison Mr. Whipple. Would she do it for $500? She answered that she would not, not for the whole State, not for all the world. He laughed, jumped up and ran off. Surely she did not take this nonsense very seriously; she forgot it until later on, until early May. The day after this scene Strang bought more arsenic, a dollar's worth (the least they would sell at Meigs' drug store) but it was never used. After his confession, they found it where he told them to look, behind a brace in back of the tool house.

Early in April John Whipple talked of going home to Vermont on the early morning stage that left between 2 and 3 A.M. Elsie urged Strang to waylay her husband at the foot of Sedgwick's Hill, fifty rods north of Cherry Hill, with an ax or a club or with one of Whipple's own pistols. But he had no appetite for meeting Whipple face to face and all he could reply was, "I will think of it."

A more harebrained scheme they hatched together. They wrote letters to two men of whom they knew, offering each $300 to kill Whipple. They never sent the letters. In one instance they weren't even sure the man could "read writing."

When John Whipple was away his niece, Henrietta Patrick, occupied the same bed with Elsie and sometimes when he was home she occupied the other bed in the room. Little Abraham appears to have slept in one of the little rooms near the basement kitchen, either with Dinah or Strang. What role Henrietta Patrick played in the family is not entirely clear. Was she supposed to keep an eye on the erratic, unreliable Elsie? If she was a companion, why did Elsie need a companion from her husband's family, in the midst of her own? Furthermore, Henrietta went in to town each day where she worked as a seamstress. She did not take care of Abraham. It may be that the Whipples were providing lodging for a poor relative who had been drawn to city life. For whatever reason she may have come to Cherry Hill, it was to be Henrietta Patrick who provided an important link in the chain of events that lay ahead.

While Elsie and Strang had been concentrating on murdering Whipple, that wasn't the only thing on their minds. Certainly they thought they were in love, and certainly they wanted each other but a house filled with eighteen people is not an easy place for trysts.

Once when John Whipple and George Wilson, the other hired man, were both away Elsie was to have come to Strang's room but Maria Van Rensselaer (the eighteen-year-old sister of Abraham) bolted a little door to the back stair that it was necessary for Elsie to pass through to get down to his room unobserved. He waited for her in vain. Early in the morning he took wood to her room as usual to make a fire. He found her awake and Henrietta asleep. They slipped out of the room into an unoccupied room on the north side of the house. There, in the words of his *Confession,* "the first criminal intercourse ensued that ever took place between us."

Later Henrietta Patrick remembered a time when Elsie was called up in the night, presumably to see to little Abraham. She was gone for half an hour and never mentioned what was the matter with the boy. Henrietta purported not to know who called Elsie, but the implications are very clear. Thereafter, little Abraham was kept upstairs. One wonders at whose suggestion.

A few days after the early morning episode Whipple returned; this would be about the 8th or 9th of April;

at ten o'clock on the 13th he left for Kingston. That same day Strang went to the livery stable of Charles Conklin on South Ferry to engage a horse and carriage to take to Troy the next day at 4 P.M.

On the morning of the 14th, a Saturday, Strang told Abraham Van Rensselaer (for whom he was now working at 50¢ a day) that he wanted to go to Troy that day to get $500 which had been deposited in a bank there in his name. He had talked of this before—the 300 acres he owned in Ohio, the business affairs that were part of this day laborer's gossamer of dreams. The business might detain him until next morning. He left Cherry Hill about ten o'clock.

In the meanwhile Elsie had announced that she was going to the city for the day to get a dress cut and would spend the night in her Columbian Hotel. This coincidence of absences might not have been noticed in so busy a household but for one of those carelessnesses that inevitably lead to the conclusion that unconsciously the sinners wished to be found out. In making the bed where she and Elsie had slept, Henrietta Patrick discovered a paper under Elsie's pillow, "a kind of letter" which read something like this: "I will meet you at the yellow house, to go to Lansingburgh, in the north part of the city, and wait till I come." Henrietta said nothing to Elsie about her discovery, rather she took the paper to Maria Matilda, Abraham Van Rensselaer's aunt who lived with her mother on the north side of the house. Maria Matilda burned it that day but now a senior member of the family had a pretty good idea of what was going on. Children had carried notes back and forth, Dinah may have seen more than she told, Henrietta had seen Strang light Elsie's pipe while she was still in bed. But now one of the family's inner circle was aware that something was afoot.

Elsie went in to town, oblivious of her own careless-ness, and headed for the Columbian Hotel where Strang, who had been loitering around about the city, caught sight of her on the front stoop about two o'clock. While she walked north on South Market Street (Broadway), he went by way of the back streets until they met at the corner of Beaver. They agreed that she would go to her old friend Mrs. Gitty Sandford at Patroon (Clinton Avenue) and North Pearl Streets where he would pick her up in the gig.

At four o'clock when he arrived at Conklin's the gig that he thought he had reserved was already rented to someone else. A gig was what the occasion called for; it was the sports car of the era. The only vehicle he could get was a farm wagon with black chassis and a green box, the equivalent of a pickup truck, hardly the vehicle for a romantic escapade. It was threatening rain so he borrowed an umbrella.

About the time Strang arrived at Conklin's, Elsie arrived at the home of Gitty Sandford, who had known her since she was a little girl. Gitty wanted to know where she was going. She said she was going to Troy with Mr. Whipple's brother but she wasn't very explicit what she would be doing there—although she dropped a hint for the imaginative: "Oh my God, I'm going riding. I don't want to go, but if I don't go, the devil will kill me!" John's brother was Barnum Whipple, a man now forty-seven years old and the successful river boat captain. Under the circumstances a brother-in-law was not a bad red herring; outsiders would be more cautious about inquiring into the whys and where-fores.

At five o'clock, however, it was no river captain who drove up to Sandford's where Elsie was waiting on the stoop, dressed in her stylish riding habit of mixed shades of lilac, covering a black bombazine dress. It was the hired man in a farm wagon with an umbrella. They went off together, driving north on the road to Troy until they came to the noble estate of the Good Patroon, Stephen Van Rensselaer, where they turned northwest for about seven miles to the Troy-Schenectady turnpike (now Route 7). It was raining hard when they got to Yearsley's public house and they pulled in there, order-ing hay for the horse and drinks for themselves.

After sunset, the rain let up and they started out again, westward toward Schenectady for about two miles when out of the west came a dark and ominous thundercloud; lightning was all about them. They turned back in a downpour and went full speed half a mile to a tavern they had passed after they left Yearsley's. They were drenched when they came to James Hill's door and be-spoke lodging for the night.

As they ate supper, Elsie rattled away to the Hills: They lived in Schenectady. They were en route to New York by steamer and sent their baggage on ahead. They were delayed by a sick child. Then she made some fumbling explanation of why they were going to Albany from Schenectady by the long way around. However, there were still questions in the minds of James and Frances Hill and of those who worked for them: The strange disparity between her fine clothes and his workingman's best suit. And the differences in class and education would have been noticed. Be this as it may, to Nancy Montgomery, Mrs. Hill's niece, Elsie Whipple and Jesse Strang looked very young and very fond of each other. They were asked if they were man and wife and they said they were.

After they had eaten they retired to a bedroom with two beds but in the morning only one was tumbled. They rose at dawn and started out for Albany. Strang left Elsie at Mrs. Sandford's and returned the horse and wagon to the livery stable, paying the rental with change from a $5 bill Elsie had stolen from her husband's pocketbook. He was back at Cherry Hill by 8 A.M. By prearrangement, Henrietta Patrick met Elsie at the Columbian Hotel where she said she had spent the night.

The lovers were pleased with themselves and each other. On the return trip they talked of her getting $100 from Fobes while Whipple was away and then eloping to Montreal. The time for this kind of impractical dreaming was over; they wanted each other but they also wanted the money that only the death of John Whipple would release. After the night at Hill's, they knew what they had to do.

5. The Excursion

On April 14, 1827, Jesse Strang, driving a horse and wagon, picked up Mrs. Whipple at 5 P.M. at her friend Gitty Sandford's. They drove to Yearsley's public house, then headed for Schenectady, but a storm caused them to spend the night at Hill's tavern. They returned the next day to Albany.

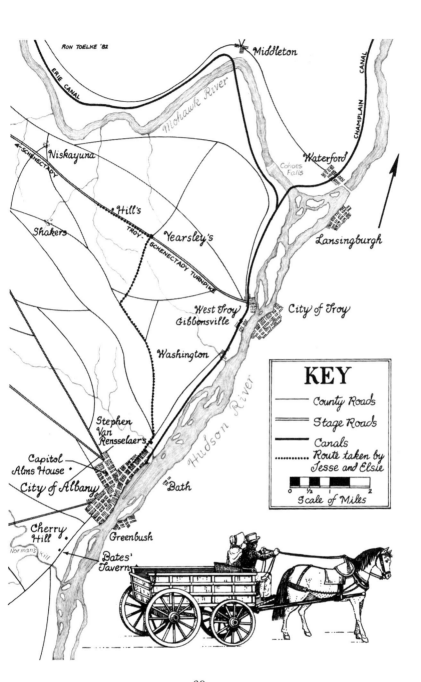

RON TOELKE '82

ERIE CANAL

Middleton

CHAMPLAIN CANAL

Mohawk River

Niskayuna

SCHENECTADY

Waterford

Cohoes Falls

Hill's

Shakers

Yearsley's

Lansingburgh

TROY-SCHENECTADY TURNPIKE

West Troy
Gibbonsville

City of Troy

Washington

Hudson River

KEY

—— County Roads

═══ Stage Roads

━━ Canals

········ Route taken by
Jesse and Elsie

0   ½   1   2

Scale of Miles

Stephen
Van
Rensselaer's

Capitol
Alms House

City of Albany

Bath

Cherry
Hill

Norman's Kill

Greenbush

Dates'
Tavern

CHAPTER 3

Preparation

THE Montreal scheme was soon forgotten and their fertile imaginations turned toward two very practical objectives. The first was to establish in the minds of as many people as possible the belief that there were prowlers about Cherry Hill who had it in for John Whipple; the second was to get a rifle and the ammunition for it. They collaborated in these designs, Strang the more active in spreading the rumor, Elsie putting on the pressure to procure the rifle. This would occupy the three weeks between April 15 and May 7.

Just when the myth about prowlers was first hatched is not clear, but it would appear to have been about the 20th of April. His story was that men were seen lurking about the premises late at night. He talked about this in the kitchen where the whole family became aware of it. Dinah thought he was trying to scare her; Abraham

Van Rensselaer was given the impression they were not interested in him. The theme must have seemed an obsession to the others; Strang's guess that these were men from the Delaware and Hudson Canal who probably had a grudge against Whipple was not taken very seriously at Cherry Hill, but a loaded rifle was kept over the kitchen door. One day when he was on the hill immediately in back of the house with William Wilson, Strang looked toward one of the second story windows and said they were in a fine place from which to shoot into the house. Wilson remarked that was a foolish thing to think about but he didn't forget it, either.

Elsie, meanwhile, was playing the same game. Idling in her Columbian Hotel about April 23, she chatted with Starr Foot, the bartender. Had he heard from Mr. Whipple? He had not. She said there were people lurking about the house and she couldn't think what for unless it was to waylay John and kill him. "I'll bet you a hat that he'll be killed." Foot, with the calm tolerance of his craft, asked if she knew of anyone who wanted to kill him, and she said, "No." It was, as he observed at her trial, a foolish remark.

While Strang and Elsie were busy fixing suspicion on the non-existent prowlers, they were also engaged in careful, tested preparation for the murder. In this their fecklessness was replaced by a thoroughness and steadfastness of purpose one could hardly have foreseen.

John Whipple was expected back in town early in May. Elsie suggested to Strang that he take one of her husband's pistols and shoot him through the window. But, being a countryman, the only weapon he was comfortable with was a rifle, nothing less than a two-barrelled rifle. She told him to find out in town what it would cost. Shortly thereafter he and Abraham Van Rensselaer went to town to sell some old iron and together they priced rifles at Moore's, the gunsmith on Beaver Street. Double-barrelled, $60, single-barrelled at $25 and $35.

That evening in the kitchen, with the family sitting about, Elsie asked Strang if he had inquired as to the price of socks while he was in town. "Yes, *sixty* cents."

"That's very dear."

He told her those were the cheapest ones, the best kind were a hundred and twenty cents. A few days later she wrote him that she would get $30 from a merchant named Daniel Winne, the balance from Fobes. About the time Strang began to spread the story about the prowlers, he picked up some confidence and told her he might be able to succeed with a single-barrelled rifle and that he could get one for $25.

On May 2 Elsie went to Fobes and asked for some money. He gave her a five-dollar bill and a $20 bill issued by The Phoenix Bank of Hartford, Connecticut. An alert business man always noted which bank stood behind the money that came to hand, for some were far more creditable than others. Furthermore, a $20 bill was probably as uncommon in daily transactions as a $100 bill would be today. Fobes gave the bill to Starr Foot, the bartender, who gave it to Elsie, sometime between 10 A.M. and 1 P.M., because Fobes was to remember that the steamboat had left the dock. Elsie gave it to Strang who used it to buy the rifle from Edward Fay; Fay later paid the bill out to Spencer Stafford. Stafford put it in a bundle with other bills, but only one other was a $20, and that from a Harrisburg bank. In August, Dr. Charles D. Townsend was in Court with the bill from Hartford ready to swear that he had received it from Stafford. The testimony of these gentlemen would prove beyond all question that Elsie Whipple was an accomplice of Strang's in the shooting of her husband.

Strang, as we have seen, found the gun he was satisfied with in Edward Fay's gunshop on Beaver Street. It was a gun Fay knew well; he had bought a dozen gunlocks from Meachum and put his name on them and this was the only one he had sold. Besides, every stock was a little different and this had its own peculiarity. He had sold it once before and the purchaser had returned it. It was a gun he could pick out of a thousand. Later he remembered that Strang was wearing a surtout coat when he came in and it was very full in the breast.

The rifle cost $15 and Fay gave Strang a $3 bill and a $2 bill in change. On the way home he bought some sugar toys at March's grocery store for the children at Cherry Hill, hiding the rifle out of doors at the end of the grocer's house. At night he recovered it, secreting it in the loft of the necessary. Elsie had given him a $5 bill along with the $20; the next day he told her the rifle was $16 and gave her the change. She sent Henrietta Patrick off immediately to buy her two yards of lace for $6.

Sunday, May 6, was a busy day for the conspirators. Whipple was expected momentarily. Because it was Sunday, Strang was more free to follow his own devices. As usual, they met in the kitchen in the morning. He remarked that when, recently, he had shot a dog for Abraham, the gun had kicked badly. She was afraid the

6. *Map of Albany in 1827*
Key

1. State Capitol
2. Jail
3. Site of execution
4. Albany Academy
5. St. Peter's Episcopal Church
6. First Dutch Church
7. Columbian Hotel, 559 South Market Street
8. Sheldon & Sykes, merchants, 456 South Market Street
9. Charles Conklin's livery stable, corner of Church and Ferry Streets
10. John Moore, gunsmith, 8 Beaver Street
11. Edward Fay, gunsmith, 16 Beaver Street
12. Mrs. Gitty Sandford, corner of Patroon and North Pearl Streets
13. R. M. Meigs, druggist, 466 South Market Street
14. F. H. Crosby's hotel, corner of South Pearl and Beaver Streets
15. Lancaster Academy

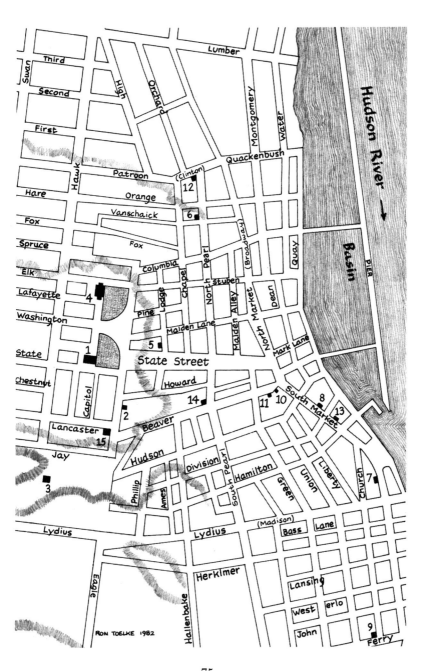

Swan
Third
Second
First
Hare
Fox
Spruce
Elk
Lafayette
Washington
State
Chestnut
Lancaster
Jay
Lydius

Hawk
High
Orchard
Patroon
Orange
Vanschaick
Fox
Columbia
Pine
Lodge
Chapel
Capitol

Lumber
Montgomery
Water
Quackenbush
(Clinton)
North Pearl
(Broadway)
Quay
North stuben
Malden Alley
North Market
Dean
Mark Lane
Malden Lane

State Street

Howard
Beaver
Hudson
Division
Phillip
Ames
South Pearl
Hamilton
Green
Union
Liberty
Church

Lydius
(Madison)
Bass Lane
Herklmer
Hallenbake
Lansing
West erlo
John
Ferry
Eagle

South Market

Hudson River →
Basin
PIER

12
6
4
1
5
14
2
15
3
11 10
8
13
7
9

RON TOELKE 1982

75

one he had bought would do the same thing and she also was concerned lest the bullet be deflected by the glass of the window through which he now was planning to shoot. She found him three panes of glass to experiment with, leaving them under his pillow.

When he told her that he had no gunpowder but he could whittle the balls, she went to the room of William Wilson, got a powderhorn. He poured some of the powder out in a paper and put the horn back where she directed him.

She wanted to know where he would experiment with the gun, so she could join him after church, in case he had not returned. While he whittled three bullets from the stock of a riding whip, she was dressing. He made no effort to hide his activity; the family all saw what he was doing and he remarked to Abraham that it was the softest lead he had ever seen. Elsie and all the family then went off to church.

Taking the glass, the bullets, the powder and after getting the rifle from the necessary, he went eighty rods into the woods and tried experiments at various distances and with various thicknesses of glass. At seven rods (the distance from the barn loft to Whipple's room) he came within an inch of the mark. He returned to the barn where he hid the rifle between the ceiling and the siding of the stable, then he went into the kitchen where the family had returned from church. The account given here of the purchase and the testing of the rifle, the procurement of the accoutrements of murder, is based on Strang's *Confession;* as we shall see, Elsie denied much of this but, to my mind, not very convincingly.

Elsie was full of questions—presumably whispered to

him in the midst of the crowded room. Did he try the gun? Yes. Did it kick? No. Did the balls glance? No. Could she see the gun? He would put it against the doorpost in the stable and leave the stable unlocked. He went out and placed it where he promised; she went out and soon came back having found it. She asked if it were loaded. No. Did she touch it? No. Then he went to the barn and put it back in its hiding place. After dinner he whittled a new bullet but it was too small to fill up the rifle—but he loaded it anyway.

When the rest of the family went to the afternoon church service, Elsie stayed behind. They met in the garden and went together to the barn where they made love. This was the last time.

That Sunday night John Whipple returned from Kingston. He stopped to see Fobes at the Columbian and pick up his mail. There were three letters, one from Vermont, one from Elsie, one from New Jersey. He tore up Elsie's without opening it. Foot, the bartender, asked him why he did that and he remarked laconically that he knew where it came from; the action, it seems to me, of a man who felt that whatever his wife might have on her mind was of no importance. Actually, the letter was full of news of the prowlers. He took up the letter from New Jersey where Elsie's grandmother lived. As he was opening the envelope he remarked that they wanted him to repair a house down there but he'd never get his money for the work, as the old lady would never die. He read the letter and said, "By God, she *is* dead." Then he walked the mile to Cherry Hill.

CHAPTER 4

The Murder

MONDAY, May 7, 1827. In the morning Elsie came into the kitchen carrying a black vest her husband had bought in New York. As Strang remembered it later on, she remarked to him, with what seems a remarkable matter-of-factness, "Last night was a good time to have killed John, if we had only known he was coming home." Strang knew better because William Wilson had been in and out of the house and barn before and after Whipple appeared.

Elsie went out and returned with a lead ball in her hand. "Mr. Whipple is loading his pistol to save his life; I have taken the last ball he had left for you to kill him with. What a wicked creature I am!" She handed it to him and he put it in his pocket.

Whipple himself came into the kitchen; obviously Elsie had been filling his ears with stories of the imaginary prowlers.

"Joseph [i.e. Strang], what does all this mean about those men being about the house so late an hour of the night? Perhaps they are after me and my money; they may get me but they won't get much money. Joseph, why don't you shoot them?"

Strang said they were keeping a loaded gun over the door for that purpose, but, he went on, "Mr. Whipple, you generally come home in the night and I might make a mistake and shoot you."

"When I come home in the night, I come directly in the house. I don't lurk about it." Then the tone changed; Whipple began to take the whole thing much less seriously and to take Strang less seriously. "Joseph, do you shoot them in the legs and if you can't shoot them in the legs, shoot 'em in the head, so you can get a chance to shake hands with them and see who they are."

After this there was talk of Strang going to work for Whipple in Kingston, and apparently a bargain was struck sometime later in the day. After breakfast Strang worked in the fields until noon when he returned, feeding his horses and then going to the kitchen for dinner. Elsie was there wanting to know whether he had loaded his rifle with the ball she had given him. He told her he would do it that afternoon.

Before eating he went back to the barn, took his rifle into the woods where he shot the too-small bullet into a "yellow pine bush six inches in diameter." Then he went back to the barn, whittled the ball she had given him down to the appropriate size. He had no patch but he forced the ball down without one, using but a small charge of powder. He had found in the hayloft a quantity of cannonballs, bombshells and fire rockets, presumably left over from the War of 1812. There he selected a good flint and completed the preparation of his gun, then returned to dinner. That afternoon he sat around the kitchen repairing locks from Bates' tavern, which the Van Rensselaers owned.

Elsie came in and sat down by him. Was the gun ready? Yes. Where did he intend to shoot from? If Whipple were on the second floor, from the roof of the shed that ran along the back of the house. Elsie agreed to roll up the window curtain as a signal indicating where her husband was, and to put him in full view.

They arranged for her to get him a pair of Whipple's heavy white socks, which she would put under Strang's pillow. They discussed what he would do with the gun after the shooting. After a while he finished with the locks and went to the barn, bringing out the horses to the well in the courtyard behind the house to water them. It was raining and everyone else was in the house. Elsie stuck her head out of the hall window on the second floor and asked if she should throw the socks down to him. He replied that she should put them under his pillow, as they had agreed, otherwise they would be discovered. She then told him that there was talk of Whipple spending the evening with old Mrs. Philip Van Rensselaer in the north side of the house. Would that make any difference? Strang would put a stick against the kitchen stoop; if Whipple went to the north end of the house, she was to put an old shoe on it; if, on the other hand, Whipple, who was not feeling very well, went to bed, she was to put a white cloth on the stick. This whole conversation took place with Strang at the well in the yard while that silly woman talked to him from the upper floor. Why no one heard them in that house full of people, it is impossible to say.

Back in the kitchen, later on, she borrowed a pencil from Abraham Van Rensselaer to write a note saying to throw the gun as far as possible if any of the family should come out.

Miss Patrick came into that bustling room with its perpetual flow of life. Strang told her he had decided to go to Kingston to work for Whipple; could she make him a pair of pantaloons that week. She could not. Well and good, he would go uptown that evening and get them there.

Whipple came in and told him, "If you see any of those men about the house, be sure to shoot them." It is obvious that nobody about the house took the prowlers story too seriously, least of all Whipple.

It must have been almost evening when Abraham Van Rensselaer came in to ask Strang what would be good for a horse that had been kicked that afternoon. Oil of spike. So Van Rensselaer gave him sixpence to get some when he went to town. From Dinah he got a phial to put it in. He went to his bedroom just off the kitchen, put on his peacoat, looked under his pillow and found the socks Elsie had brought him, put those in the pocket of his peacoat and went off to town.

He had time to waste before it was truly dark. He went to Sheldon & Sykes' store on South Market Street, about a mile from Cherry Hill. He bought cloth and trimmings for his pantaloons. There was palaver over what kind of buttons he would buy, wood or horn, finally settling on the latter. Then they went over his account. Then there was a long conversation about a sixpence piece

7. Bird's-eye View of Cherry Hill

A yard is between the house and the barn. The Whipples' window overlooks the south (right) end of the shed that runs along the back of the house. A deep ravine and stream (not in the drawing) is to the northwest. See also Illustration 2 on page 97.

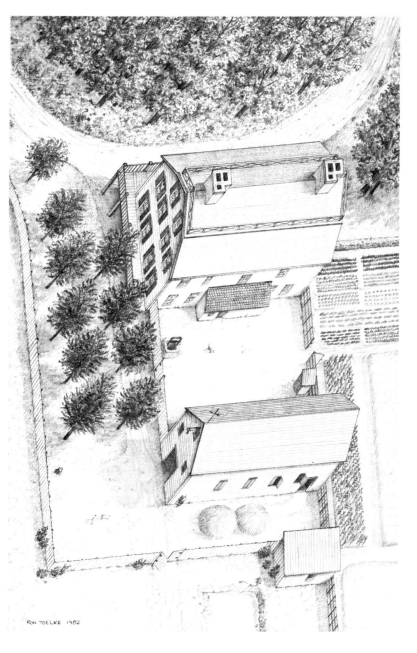

RON TOELKE 1982

83

which had been cut in two and then tied together with a thread. The clerk went outside and closed the shutters; Strang stayed on. It was well after nine o'clock now. He went to Meigs' druggist shop and got sixpence worth of spike. Then he stopped at a tailor shop to see if he could get his pantaloons cut. As he foresaw, it was too late. He was, of course, establishing his presence in town; his dawdling, his garrulous, easy conversations, his relaxed aimlessness would all help to establish an alibi, if somewhere along the line something went wrong. As a potential murderer, his actions were, at this point, exemplary. Calculating accurately, sure of his procedures, unafraid, no babbling about what was really on his mind. At this point he had the courage of his depravity and, if he had traveled further along this road, he might have made it.

Now speed was of the essence. He zigzagged from South Market (Broadway) to South Pearl Street. At Cherry Hill he went into the front courtyard and peered in the southeast kitchen window. There was Elsie sitting in a corner smoking her pipe; around the fire were Maria Van Rensselaer (Abraham's eighteen-year-old sister), Henrietta Patrick and Dinah Jackson. He checked the stick he had placed by the stoop before he went to town; there was neither cloth nor old shoe on it. He went to the southwest of the house, up the steep rise of land and could see the widow Catharine (Abraham and Maria's mother) sewing in her bedroom, which had apparently been moved to the first floor after her husband's death, occupying what is now the dining room.

Strang went to the loft of the barn where he could

see somebody sitting in Whipple's room but he couldn't distinguish who. He went to the stable, got his rifle and proceeded to the northwest corner of the lot, by the board fence, below some cherry trees about ten rods (165') from the house, pulled off his boots and socks, put on Whipple's heavy socks that Elsie had got him, took off his peacoat, wrapped his purchases in it, laid it in a corner by the side of the fence. He went now, wearing the socks for silence, unburdened except for the rifle, to a wood box about four feet high. This he moved to the northwest corner of the shed which was attached to the rear of the house. This shed was eight feet wide and ran for twenty feet along the west side of the house to which it was attached.

He now climbed on the wood box, placed the rifle in the eaves trough, with the aid of an iron hook nailed to the post he climbed silently onto the roof of the shed. He walked to the south end of the shed and peeked into the window; Elsie had kept her promise and raised the curtain for a better view. There sat Whipple with his back to the window, about nine feet away. Abraham Van Rensselaer was sitting opposite him in a low rocking chair; they were going over some accounts.

Now, sure of the setup, Strang went back to the eaves trough, got the rifle, opened the pan of the lock, took a paper he had previously put over the priming to keep it dry, shut the pan, cocked the rifle, put the muzzle close to the sash. Strang was standing erect now. Van Rensselaer's face was out of sight. He took deliberate aim under Whipple's left arm with as much composure as if he were shooting at a deer. He fired and heard

85

8. *Woodcut of the Murder of John Whipple*

This woodcut appears on the title page of the pamphlet, *Trial, Sentence, and Confession of Jesse Strang for the Murder of John Whipple,* New York, C. Brown, 1827. See Bibliography, page 118.

Whipple cry out, "Oh Lord!" For a fraction of a second Van Rensselaer saw a white face that he did not recognize at the window.

Strang backed up a few steps, slipped, flung the rifle, fell to the ground, sprang to his feet, saying, "Thank God, I'm not hurt," grabbed the rifle and ran to the north gate in the courtyard which surrounded the rear of the house. He ran down the hill to the place where he had left his jacket and bundle, threw them over the fence along with the rifle, which stuck with the muzzle in the ground. It was Strang's impression that all this had taken place less than fifteen minutes after he left Sheldon & Sykes, where he bought the cloth. A careful retracing and timing of his actions leads one to think it more likely that it was half an hour, but not much more. It was now about ten o'clock.

Inside Cherry Hill pandemonium broke loose. Catharine Van Rensselaer shrieked. Down in the kitchen Henrietta Patrick had been making molasses candy. She and Maria clung to Dinah, then with Elsie briefly hid themselves in Dinah's room, thinking there were robbers in the house. Van Rensselaer and Whipple rose up after the shot and headed for the stairs. At the top step John Whipple dropped dead. Abraham came to the kitchen, which was again full of children and women. He told them what had happened. There on a bench, a little apart, sat Elsie, her pipe in her hand. Dinah went out of the house calling the dog, a dog who let no stranger approach the house without barking, but who paid no attention to those he knew. There he was in his little shed on the south side of the house—calm and unperturbed.

To the west and north of Cherry Hill was a deep ravine where a stream flowed, and still probably flows now beneath the surface of First Avenue. There Strang buried his rifle in the sandy mud, stamped on it and covered it with leaves. He pulled off Whipple's socks, put on his own, his boots and coat, started off, bundle under his arm; then he remembered the telltale socks and went back to bury them at the bottom of the ravine. He climbed up out of the ravine, worked his way across lots until he came to South Pearl Street, a quarter mile north of Cherry Hill. He saw some people hurrying toward the house and, slipping out of the shadows, he followed them, his bundle under his arm, the picture of questioning innocence.

When Strang arrived at Cherry Hill there were three or four men by the gate and another one or two by the stoop, trying to get in the front door which was probably little used. He went to the kitchen door, beneath the stoop. Dinah Jackson opened it. "Is that you, Doctor?" "Yes." "Come in. Mr. Whipple is shot." He threw his bundle down and went to the head of the stairs where Whipple lay in the hall, just north of the room where he had been shot. The body was at the top landing, the feet and legs a foot over the first step. Looking at the body, looking at his accomplished design, Jesse Strang turned pale, or, as Abraham Van Rensselaer testified, "White as a sheet or a ghost." And later it seemed to him that this was when he first suspected Strang but he said nothing to anyone "because Strang was one of the family."

At Van Rensselaer's order, he went out with a gun and looked around the grounds. Then at the widow Catharine's order he unfastened her shutters, that the windows be safely closed. By that time a physician had come and certified that Whipple was dead. Strang was sent to town to find Mr. Frederich, the coroner. He went to town, to Frederich's house, to a bar, he sent a man to the theatre, all to no avail, except that another coroner, Thomas L. Pemberton, was flushed out and came down to Cherry Hill. In the meantime, Strang, following orders, went by the Columbian Hotel to tell Fobes the news.

When he returned to Cherry Hill he was immediately sworn in as one of the jurors in the coroner's inquest. The body was taken to a front room in the second story where it was undressed and the wound discovered. Then they agreed to adjourn until 9 A.M. the next day. Soon afterward Strang was sent on some errand to "the old lady's room," old Maria Sanders Van Rensselaer. Away from her Aunt Catharine, away from Maria, away from Henrietta Patrick, away from Dinah Jackson, there was Elsie with the old lady. The lovers said nothing to each other. That night young Abraham Van Rensselaer shared Jesse Strang's bed, presumably because Whipple's corpse was in Abraham's room, the southeast bedroom his parents had formerly occupied. The sleeping must have been fitful for everyone at Cherry Hill that night.

CHAPTER 5

Aftermath

THE morning after the murder, Strang was sent to the city to get Dr. Joel A. Wing to come to Cherry Hill and extract the bullet. On the way back Strang kept talking about those mysterious prowlers. Somebody from down river, no doubt; Strang had seen two of them himself.

The coroner's jury reconvened and Strang, while a member of the jury, also testified before them. He was zealous to fix the guilt on strangers, so zealous that the coroner was suspicious. Strang paced about the room, looked out the window, showed not the slightest interest in the bullet which fascinated everyone else on the jury.

Later he was on a bench in the kitchen. Elsie asked if the gun and socks were safely hidden. All taken care of. Soon the police sent for him, seeking particulars about the prowlers. He said that he had seen a man headed north on Pearl Street away from the house just after the murder. But this proved to be Kilian Van Rensselaer, Abraham's uncle, who left his gun at Milligan's grocery store. Strang's timetable for Monday night was confirmed by the clerk at Sheldon & Sykes where he bought the cloth, who said it would have been impossible for him to have committed the murder.

The next afternoon, for the first time, he and Elsie were alone. "They suspect you and me and talk of taking us up," she told him. A moment later Abraham called him out of the kitchen and told him he was wanted again at the police office. Someone took him there and he was committed to prison for further examination.

The questioning began in earnest. The expedition to Hill's tavern on April 14 was the thread they pulled to unravel the matter. Strang tried one lie after another but at last they showed him what they said was Elsie's affidavit, and he confessed that they had been together as man and wife. Then Fay, the gunsmith, and his journeyman called at the jail; they had Strang put his surtout coat on and the two men recognized him. Finally he was formally charged with murder.

His first move was to secure one of the aristocracy to defend him, John Van Ness Yates, Esq. He confessed that Orton was not his name, that he was from down river, that he had gone to Ohio two years before, leaving his wife under the pretense that she was unfaithful to him.

Yates wasn't interested in taking the case but Calvin Pepper was and to him Strang confessed the whole story, urging that he get the rifle before cattle exposed it.

His father and stepmother came to see him; to them he denied his guilt and urged them to get additional counsel, preferably the Honorable Thomas J. Oakley of Poughkeepsie. They told their son that if he were telling the truth they would see that no money was wanting to defend him. Soon Pepper had a letter from Oakley agreeing to join the defense.

Strang's counsel were able men. Calvin Pepper was thirty-one years old, had had responsibility for the 1820 census in Albany (10,541 residents), and was an active lawyer and politician of the Martin Van Buren persuasion. Since 1823 he had been the State Librarian and, in that post, able to satisfy both Van Buren and Governor De Witt Clinton. The Honorable Thomas J. Oakley had been leader of the Assembly and State Attorney General, a Clintonian stalwart who would close his career as Chief Justice of the Superior Court in New York City, a city where his son, known as "Elegant Oakley," would be Mayor. By a curious coincidence, Oakley Sr. had in 1818 introduced the legislation which established the State Library, now directed by Calvin Pepper.

The arrest of Strang frightened Elsie profoundly. Throughout Tuesday she had been in good control of herself, but when Strang was taken back to the police office on Wednesday, when suppertime came and went and he did not return, and then when word came that he had been arrested, she went all to pieces. She had not been popular in that house; as Henrietta Patrick remarked, she was more sociable with Strang, the hired man, than with the rest of the family; nobody else was so sociable with him as she. She must have been a very

93

uncomfortable woman to have about the house, what with her intense egocentrism, her tears, her tempers, her failure to live up to the manners of her class.

Wednesday night she and Maria woke Abraham up to ask about Strang. It couldn't be, she insisted, that his replies differed from hers. Had they found $500 in his trunk? No, only clothes and rum. It had been a hard day for her; the repeated examinations by the police of her Aunt Caty (Abraham's mother), of whom she was afraid, unnerved her and at one point she had fainted. They called the older woman to come to her, but she refused. Aunt Caty suspected too much, had said to Elsie that she was a bad woman and might possibly hang. Aunt Caty never testified at the trial but one is conscious of her presence and her long-standing disapproval of her niece.

Another time that same day she was sitting with her husband's corpse when a gentleman asked if she would uncover his face and kiss it. She was indignant and asked him if he thought her afraid to kiss her own husband. Whereupon she put her arms around John's neck and kissed him. When nothing untoward happened, the gentleman said, "Now I am satisfied." The bier kiss is an ancient test of those accused of murder; if the murderer can bring himself to kiss the corpse, the wounds will bleed.

Aunt Caty's daughter, Maria, describing her cousin Elsie at this stage of the tragedy, went into particulars about her personality: "She is a weakly, sickly person, when always complaining shows her nervous affections very plainly, complaining more than she was ailing. Easily discouraged—at times low spirits—at other times as light as a feather, as you may say." Maria comes through as a very clear-headed young woman.

Thursday was the day of the funeral and there was a kind of endless hysterical flow coming from Elsie. Always a compulsive talker, she chattered, wept, fainted, postured, begged for sympathy; she was all alone in the world and her own relatives were intimating she was the cause of her husband's death. She defended Strang to everyone to whom she talked. He was one of her husband's best friends, John had hired him the very day of the murder at $16 a month, a dollar more than he was getting; had agreed to pay for some new clothes for him. She wished she were dead; she wished they would make John's grave wide enough for her, too. To the family physician, Dr. Joel A. Wing, she said, "My Aunt, my Uncle Knickerbacker [Herman Knickerbacker], and most of the family are lowering upon me, intimating as much as that I am the cause of . . . my husband's death. Everyone seems turned my enemy."

John Whipple had a nephew, Melancton Whipple, who had dined with him at Fobes' the day of the murder. For about ten days thereafter he was in and out of Cherry Hill, frequently talking to Elsie, and one can trace, through those conversations, the breaking down of her defenses. The day of the funeral she told him, as she had told others, that Strang was one of John's best friends. One day she told him about getting money from Fobes because Strang had asked to borrow $20. A few days later she said to Melancton that she had been told Strang had said he had been somewhere and stayed with her. It was a lie. No such thing. A few days later her theme was that Strang had lied and would lie again. Now she told him that Strang had said he would have her, if it cost him his life; that he proposed going to Canada with her. Later, that Strang had threatened to take Whipple's life. Again, she asked, if Strang were convicted, would he be brought to testify against her? By this time Melancton was convinced she was guilty and saw no more of her.

On May 25 Elsie was arrested and lodged in the Albany jail; out of humanity, Henrietta Patrick's mother, John Whipple's sister, was permitted to spend the night in her cell. The next day Elsie made a voluntary statement, a web of truths, lies and half-truths. Whether Elsie could distinguish among these shades of veracity is a nice question. Strang had told her he would poison Mr. Whipple but he never gave her any arsenic to administer; he told her he would waylay Mr. Whipple "and that if he was found out in it, he would get her as deep in the mud as he was in the mire." She had told Whipple of this threat and he laughed at it. Both of these declarations of Strang were some considerable time before the murder, and before she went riding with Strang. On that occasion they stayed together at a tavern and she was imprudent. She had been deluded by Strang but is innocent of murder and cannot swear that Strang is guilty of murder. She denied any role in the experiments with glass and bullets; she never gave him a bullet and he never asked for one. He had asked for the loan of a pair of white socks, which she got for him; she did this innocently, merely trying to accommodate him. There was a golden heart it was claimed he gave her; on the contrary, she bought it from him for $3. He never asked for $60; nor any other money except on the occasion when she lent him $20—with the innocent intention of obliging him. As for the window curtain in the room where John Whipple was shot, he himself had thrown it aside as he wanted light in the room in the morning. She never drew it aside nor fastened it up. To all this she swore before Magistrate John O. Cole.

The grand jury met June 12 and visited Strang in jail, both in a body and in small groups. They found a bill against him, they hold him that Elsie had testified enough to hang him. They had threatened, cajoled, begged and warned him in a steady stream. He had lost his appetite; he was sleeping badly; they said Elsie had confessed. Maybe she would have enough influence to get them off lightly. For forty-eight hours his confidence waned until, about 10 P.M. on the 14th, he sent for Becker, the jailer, and confessed.

He told Becker that he was guilty but that Elsie was at the bottom of it all. He told him where the rifle, arsenic, socks, window glass and rifle balls were to be found. That night Becker went out to see what he could find, only to come back empty-handed. About 8 A.M., Pepper, Becker and Coroner Pemberton came to the cell and Strang asked Pepper to go with them and get the evidence. An hour later that were back with the rifle and the arsenic. Mid morning they took Strang out of jail, followed by a large crowd; they located the glass on the ground, the lead still in the tree. Then they went to the shallow ravine where the rifle had been found, thence to the deep ravine to the north, but the socks they could not, nor ever did, find.

By this time Elsie was lodged in the third floor of the jail, two cells away from Strang. Instead of being chained to her cell, like Strang, she was free to move about. It was hot and the door was left open. Becker's thirteen-year-old daughter, Matilda, was there to keep her company. She went down the hall on several occasions to lie on the floor and talk to Strang through the inch-and-a-half crack under his door. She blamed him for confessing; if he had held his tongue they could both have gotten clear. He had given her a hand-written poem about them both, supposedly written by himself, but a few days later the assistant jailer told her it was copied from the *National Observer.* Elsie said she thought it likely; Strang "didn't know enough to compose such a piece of poetry as that."

Strang was convinced that if Elsie were convicted with him, the powerful influence of her friends might persuade the Governor to commute their punishments and that they might both escape public execution. He dreamed up ideas to strengthen the case against her which he discussed with Pepper but the next day Pepper and Edward Livingston, the District Attorney, came to his cell together. It is worth remembering that Mr. Livingston was related to the Ten Broecks, the Westerlos, the Van Rensselaers and was married to a Lansing. Livingston warned Strang not to think that by testifying against Elsie he would ingratiate himself with the authorities one whit. Nothing he might say against her would lighten his sentence, nothing would suggest a pardon. He was guilty; he must be convicted; he ought to die. Mr. Livingston was the last man on earth to recommend mercy for him. With this blow to his hopes, he decided to withdraw his confession and stand trial.

The trial of Jesse Strang began on July 25, 1827, less

than twelve weeks after the murder. The excitement generated by this case was immense. Newspapers all over the Northeast carried day-by-day accounts, not a few of them with almost complete testimony. The trial of The People vs. Jesse Strang, *alias* Joseph Orton, was held in the Assembly Chamber of the State Capitol, it being the only government hall large enough for the crowd. Carpets had been removed, cushioned chairs and desks pushed back in a very wide circle and their places occupied by simpler chairs and benches. A temporary platform held the bench for Judge William Duer and his associate judges, the Mayor of Albany, John Stevenson, James M'Kown, Recorder of the City, Judge Richard S. Treat, of the Court of Common Pleas, and an Alderman named Welcome Esleeck. In front of the bench were tables and seats for counsel, forming a semi-circle. At the right of the bench were seats for reporters and behind them, seats for witnesses. Elsie sat near the reporters, heavily veiled. Strang, dressed in a lilac-colored, mixed cloth suit, sat at the bar, resting his head on one hand, drumming with the fingers of his free hand. The Assembly Chamber, the lobbies and halls, the streets outside were all filled with the curious. It was a big show.

The jury consisted of a cordwainer (shoemaker) and a merchant, both from Albany, and ten farmers. The first witness was Abraham Van Rensselaer, who described the murder as he had seen it. He told of Strang's campaign to persuade everyone that prowlers were lurking about to shoot John Whipple. Strang had talked to him about buying a good rifle before he went to Ohio; he had boasted of his skill as a marksman. The family dog had not barked at the time of the murder. Van Rens-

9. The Trial of Jesse Strang

The trial was held in the Assembly Chamber of the State Capitol. Standing near the site of the present State Capitol, the building was designed by Philip Hooker, built in 1804-09, and demolished in 1883.

selaer had suspected Strang as early as the night of the murder.

Dr. Wing testified and then Dinah Jackson, whose freedom from slavery had come three weeks before, making it possible for her to testify. The coroner described Strang's lack of interest in the bullet extracted from Whipple's corpse.

Fay, the gunsmith, told of selling the rifle to Strang and the $20 from the Phoenix Bank of Hartford. He swore the bullet that killed Whipple would fit the rifle he sold Strang. Fobes, the manager of the Columbian Hotel, and Foot, the bartender, testified to having given that bill to Elsie. Becker identified the rifle which he had found where Strang told him to look. There was testimony about the arsenic. William Wilson, the hired man, told of Strang pointing to the window and saying that would be a fine place to shoot in. At breakfast the second morning after the murder Wilson asked Strang if he remembered that conversation. Strang had said, "Yes," and then got up from the table and went out of doors.

Then Frances Hill and her husband, James, and Nancy Montgomery, who lived at the Hills' tavern, all told of the night Strang and Elsie spent under their roof. Conklin, the livery man, told of renting out the horse and green wagon to Strang and people from Cherry Hill told of both of them being away the night of April 14.

While Frances Hill was testifying, Livingston asked her if she could positively identify Strang, who sat not three feet away. "Will you swear positively, Madam? Look at him!" Whereupon Strang turned around so as to look her full in the face, drew himself up and made a diabolical move, "his eyes seemed to light up with the sparks of hell." Mrs. Hill shuddered, choked up and burst into tears. They moved her closer to the bench and Strang moved back to his usual position with a demoniacal laugh. It was the high spot of the trial.

Then came the question of the confession and how much pressure had been exerted on Strang, and whether it should be admitted, whether John Becker should be allowed to recount Strang's statement to him and the finding of the rifle and other evidence as a result of that statement. Finally, Judge Duer allowed it and when it was out and the jury had heard it, District Attorney Livingston rested and Mr. Oakley had nothing to say.

Judge Duer charged the jury and they went out to their deliberations. In fifteen minutes they returned with the verdict: Guilty.

It was sometime that summer, perhaps just before Strang's trial, that old Maria Van Rensselaer who lived in the north side of Cherry Hill had a visit from a ten-year-old granddaughter, Catharina Van Rensselaer. One day the little girl's father, General Solomon Van Rensselaer, and the Hon. Herman Knickerbacker dropped by, paid their respects to the venerable old lady, then taking the child with them in their gig, drove to the jail at the corner of Eagle and Howard Streets and went upstairs. Nearly a half century later Catharina, now Mrs. Bonney, recalled the scene:

> At the request of the gentlemen the barriers were removed; the ponderous door being unlocked slowly moved back on its hinges, and we were in the presence of the unhappy criminal, Strang, who was chained to a

103

strong iron staple. There was a momentary gleam from his defiant eyes, and then his unquiet gaze turned again to the Bible he was reading when we entered the room. . . . After a time we went to Mrs. Whipple who had been assigned by the jailor, rooms on the same floor; she occupied an apartment adjoining Strang's. Mrs. Whipple was in a recumbent posture on her cot; dressed in an elaborately trimmed white cambric, her soft, glossy hair of extraordinary length floated over her shoulders. There was something indescribably attractive in her fair face, and indeed she looked lovely, and really seemed much distressed when she recognized her visitors. With breathless stillness I took in the whole scene, and forcibly realized the isolation and helplessness of one, who was born a lady, but had by frivolousness and vanity sold her birthright. The poor captive exerted herself to regain her self command, and resolutely checked the hysteric sobs. I remembered how, while struggling even to agony, she lifted her streaming eyes, and poured out her heart, conversing with an enthusiasm and personal power that kindled pity and heartfelt sympathy in the breasts of the gentlemen. "There is nothing that touches feeling like feeling itself," and it was honorable to humanity that her peril should have stirred these large-hearted gentlemen to vigorous exertions to save this woman from the fearful jeopardy that then seemed inevitable.

Elsie's trial began on the 30th of July, four days after Strang's was concluded. The dramatis personae was much the same, except that her principal lawyer was

Abraham Van Vechten, one of the brightest stars of the Albany bar and a relative of Elsie's. Because of his family ties, Edward Livingston, the District Attorney, was in a much more difficult spot than he had been during Strang's trial. In the opening speech Livingston said he intended to call Strang to the stand to prove the role that Elsie had played.

Abraham Van Rensselaer was again the first witness. Most of his testimony covered the days after the murder and Elsie's growing hysteria. Then his sister Maria testified to her "singular actions." "She was always subject to nervous affections, and her mother before her."

Gitty Sandford told of Elsie's visit and Frances Hill repeated her testimony that "only one bed was tumbled." Matilda Becker and the turnkey told of conversations under Strang's cell door and of the poem from the *National Observer*. Fobes testified about the $20 bill. Henrietta Patrick told of the note she found under Elsie's pillow, the note that Maria Matilda burned. Dinah Jackson and Starr Foot, the bartender, Dr. Wing, women in the household, each built the case against her a little more firmly: the love affair which provided motive, the assistance in purchasing the gun, the letters back and forth, the lies about prowlers.

Finally Livingston called Jesse Strang, whereupon Elsie's lawyer objected on the grounds that Strang had been convicted of an infamous crime and therefore was incompetent. Also, if Strang were used as a witness he must become eligible for executive clemency.

Livingston replied that it was the sentence, not the conviction, which would disqualify a witness and Strang had not yet been sentenced. Finally, he would very carefully preadmonish Strang that he was not to hope for a pardon in this world under any circumstances. By this time it was 8 P.M. on Thursday night. Judge Duer decided on a recess until the next morning when he would decide the matter.

The next morning the judge announced that the court had considered the question and had decided that there was no doubt that a person convicted of a crime but not yet sentenced was a competent witness. However, the court had further addressed itself to the question whether

on a principle of public policy, and in furtherance of public justice, the person convicted shall be permitted to testify against the accused. From the evidence before the court, it appeared that Strang meditated the murder he committed for the space of six months; that he had an illicit intercourse with the prisoner at the bar; and that he had expressed himself determined to have her if it cost him his life. He is a man of about 30 years of age, not deficient in experience, on the contrary artful and deceptive, passing himself off as an unmarried man, and under a false and assumed name. The character in which he appears before the court as to his participation in the crime which has been committed, is not as an instrument used by the prisoner to get rid of her husband, but as the seducer of the prisoner to obtain possession of her person and property. The prisoner at the bar appears as a young woman, now about 25 years of age, married at the early age of 14 to her late husband, possessed of property to a considerable amount, of a character light, frivolous, weak, vain, imprudent and wicked, and guilty to a certain degree; a fit instrument in the hands of a designing man, but destitute of those qualities which might be supposed to have swayed the mind or controlled the actions of the person with whom she had an illicit intercourse. Had the case been reversed, and she presented as a woman of experience, of strength of mind and energy of character, who had lived unhappily with her husband, and expressed a determination to get rid of him — who had selected as her paramour a youth of inexperience, and by the seductions of her person and her fortune had induced him to commit the murder, in the exercise of their discretion the court would not have hesitated to admit him as a witness, and in a full disclosure of the facts to have recommended him to mercy.

The judge therefore decided that "Jesse Strang cannot be admitted as a witness." Any further prosecution was abandoned and, without leaving their seats, the jury accommodatingly declared Elsie Whipple not guilty. The Albany Establishment had closed ranks, however distasteful it may have been to do so, and saved one of their number from the disgrace of a public hanging. The next day Strang was sentenced to be hanged by the neck until dead.

The summer of 1827 must have been one of the most exciting Albany, which has made more than its fair share of history, ever lived through. On July 4 the blacks from miles around came for a great parade and very dignified celebration of the end of slavery, with banners and sermons and an African band. In the meantime, the Strang-Whipple case was on everybody's tongue and the press of the whole country followed the trials of the two lovers. Now came the hanging, Friday, August 24.

At that time Eagle Street stopped at Jay, a block south of the prison. Beyond that point, almost as far as Lydius (now Madison) was a great ravine with the Ruttenkill flowing through it. The ravine, according to Munsell, was three hundred feet broad and fifty feet deep through most of its length. In the 1840s it would take three years, two hundred and fifty workmen and sixty teams to fill in that space, now occupied by the Mall. At the bottom of the ravine was a level, grassy area where the gallows was raised. A turn of the Ruttenkill just to the west made it possible for the gallows to be surrounded on three sides by hills, providing an intimate view of the action.

Early in the morning the roads, the steamboats, the ferries were crowded. All normal business stopped. As the day wore on somewhere between 30,000 and 40,000 persons concentrated within view of the site where Strang would play his last role. Eleven hundred vehicles are said to have entered the town from the north and 175 were left by the roadside north of the Patroon's bridge. Newspapers of the time always noted with surprise the large number of women who came to hangings; editors, I suppose, being enmeshed in the cliché about the gentler sex.

Thirteen companies of militia marched to the gallows area between 11 A.M. and noon and stood two and three deep around the structure, some of them coming from Troy, Schenectady, Bethlehem and Greenbush.

At 1:15 P.M. the jail door opened and out stepped Strang dressed in the standard garments for the occasion: loosely styled pants and rather long overdress of white, trimmed with black, black gloves and shoes, a white cap also trimmed with black. With him were Captain Osborn, the marshal, Sheriff Ten Eyck, Mr. Becker, the jailer, and the Episcopal clergyman, Reverend Mr. Lacey, escorted by the Albany Republican Artillery. Preceded by two black horses drawing a wagon with his coffin in a pine box, they marched to the place of execution.

Strang mounted the scaffold with firmness and appeared in complete control of himself and the situation. For a month now he had devoted himself to prayers and Bible reading. His father, Daniel, and his stepmother had visited him some days previous and several of his thirteen living brothers and sisters had been with him the night before. The Reverend Mr. Lacey was frequently in his cell with him.

Circulating through the crowd, along with the other hucksters usual to such occasions, were men selling a pamphlet titled *The Confession of Jesse Strang made to C. Pepper, Esq.* This had been copyrighted on August 13 and contained a foreword by Daniel Strang, authorizing the publication and guaranteeing it to contain "nothing except what said Jesse shall sanction and declare to be true at the close of his life." And, indeed, it remains the best single contemporary account of the crime.

Now Strang stepped forward and addressed the multitude. He hoped that his execution would lead them to reflect upon the effects of sin and lust. He hoped that they would depart from that place with hearts impressed with contrition, as was his. Then holding up a copy of

10. The Hanging of Jesse Strang

The hanging took place at the head of Beaver Street,
where the Empire State Plaza now stands. Strang was
escorted to the scaffold by the Albany Republican
Artillery, city officials, and Reverend Lacey A crowd
of thirty to forty thousand watched.

the *Confession* he made to Calvin Pepper, he said: "This contains a full confession of the great transaction for which I am about to die, and every single word that it contains, to the best of my knowledge, is true; if there is a single word in it that is not true, it has been inserted by mistake and not by design." He then handed the pamphlet to Mr. Lacey, having created what must be one of the greatest sales pitches of all times. The Advertising Hall of Fame should give Jesse Strang an honored place.

The last rites of the Episcopal Church were read, in which he earnestly joined. The sheriff, the jailer, Mr. Lacey all bade him farewell. At 1:45 he declared himself ready and pulled the cap down over his face. The rope was tightened around his neck, the drop fell but the job had been bungled; instead of breaking his neck neatly, he hung there until he suffocated to death. After half an hour the body was declared dead, taken down and turned over to the family to be taken to Westchester for burial.

This was the last public hanging in Albany; the crowds were too large, the mood too close to carnival. How big the crowd would have been if Elsie had made the occasion a double-header, it is hard to imagine. But Elsie was safely in New York City, where she was recognized as she strolled the streets that same afternoon. In January 1829 she married a Nathaniel Freeman in New Brunswick, New Jersey. That marriage lasted only a few years — Freeman died and Elsie moved to Onandaga County, New York, where she died in 1832.

CHAPTER 6

Four Postscripts

1. The State Museum

Strang would probably have been delighted to know that by early fall 1827 the New York State Museum, then a private institution, was advertising wax figures showing "Strang in the act of shooting Whipple—they being exact likenessess—Strang being a mould taken from his face taken by the artist Coffee [William J. Coffee, c. 1774-1846]—Whipple from a drawing by Ames [Ezra Ames, 1768-1836], moulded by Street of New Haven. The rifle that Strang has is the identical one with which he shot Whipple." *Albany Argus,* Oct. 8, 1827.

2. The Ghost

The ghost that has long been reported walking at Cherry Hill—is it Whipple or Strang? It's time to settle the matter once and for all. The ghost, if ghost there be, is Whipple. I am willing to listen to any real proof to the contrary, but my convictions are not easily shaken. As I have said elsewhere, in our folklore murder victims have a strong penchant for returning; murderers stay put.

3. ABRAHAM D. L. WHIPPLE

On May 19, 1827 Elsie, probably under pressure from her Lansing relatives, put the Columbian Hotel in trust for little Abraham. He was to have first claim on the proceeds for his maintenance and education. She would receive the surplus "free from the disposition, interference or control of any future husband she may have." Abraham grew up, studied law, sold the hotel for $15,000 in 1842 to the attorney under whom he had been studying. He died in Sterling, Virginia in 1890, when he was sixty-nine years old, and is buried beside his wife in Albany Rural Cemetery, the Valhalla of all true Albanians.

4. LEVI KELLEY

One of the thousands who drove to Albany to see Jesse Strang hanged was a farmer from Cooperstown named Levi Kelley. After the show was over and he and his companion were on the long journey home, he is said to have remarked that no one who had witnessed such a scene could ever commit murder. He would have agreed with the Albany editor who wrote, "We trust none who were witnesses of this scene will forget that this ignominious death was the consequence of an indulgence in vicious courses and criminal passions."

Eleven days later Kelley lost his temper and in an uncontrollable rage shot his hired man. He was hanged the last day of 1827. It was quite an occasion—a platform on which many of the huge crowd were standing gave way and two people were killed and twenty or thirty injured. Technically it was a much neater hanging than Strang's, but technique isn't everything. When I hear the politicians argue that a return to capital punishment will inhibit murders, I think wryly of Levi Kelley. You are free, of course, to do the same.

Bibliography

THE wide interest this case aroused is reflected, not only in the extensive press coverage from Albany, but also in the large number of pamphlets and broadsides which it encouraged. Many of these were pirated reprints. The *Confession* which Strang advertised from the gallows was *The Confession of Jesse Strang made to C. Pepper, Esq.*

The pamphlets are to be found in the New-York Historical Society library in New York City and the library of the New York State Historical Association in Cooperstown. Through the generosity of the New-York Historical Society, Cooperstown has been able to complete its file by Xeroxing.

The numbers following the name McDade refer, of course, to numbers given those itemized in the murder buff's bible, Thomas M. McDade, *Annals of Murder: A*

117

Bibliography of Books and Pamphlets on American Murders from Colonial Times to 1900. Norman, Okla.: University of Oklahoma Press, 1961.

PAMPHLETS

Trial of Jesse Strang for the Murder of John Whipple. Printed by D. M'Glashan, No. 3 Beaver St., [Albany, N.Y.], 1827. 35 pp. [McDade no. 940].

Trial and Acquittal of Mrs. Whipple . . . With a Brief Sketch of Her Life. Printed by C. Brown, 211 Water St., New York, N.Y., 1287 [sic] = [1827]. 25 pp. [McDade no. 942].

Confession of Jesse Strang made to C. Pepper, Esq. Printed by John B. Van Steenbergh, Albany, N.Y., 1827. 35 pp. [McDade no. 934].

The Authentic Confession of Jesse Strang . . . As Made to Rev. Mr. Lacey. . . . E.M. Murden & A. Ming, Jr., 4 Chambers St., New York, N.Y., 1827. 20 pp. [McDade no. 933]. Not really a confession, rather a re-cap of the trial using some materials from the Pepper confession. The Rev. Lacey claimed he had no part in it.

Trial, Sentence and Confession of Jesse Strang for the Murder of John Whipple. Printed by C. Brown, 211 Water St., New York, N.Y., 1827. 24 pp. [McDade no. 941].

Particulars Relative to the Trials of Jesse Strang and Mrs. Whipple. n.d. 16 mo. 26 pp. [Lacks title page in NYSHA copy].

Authentic Confession of Jesse Strang, Executed at Albany for Murder of John Whipple. New York, N.Y., 1827. 16 mo. 20 pp.

BIBLIOGRAPHY

Confession of Jesse Strang who was Executed at Albany August 24, 1827 for the Murder of John Whipple. Albany, N.Y., 1827. 16 mo. 24 pp.

Pictorial Life and Adventures of Mrs. Whipple: Jesse Strang, etc. By the editor of the *New York National Police Gazette.* Philadelphia: T.B. Peterson and Brothers, 1848. 16 mo. 56 pp. [McDade no. 936].

Trial and Confession of Jesse Strang for the Murder of John Whipple . . . Sentence of Death . . . Trial and Acquittal of Mrs. Whipple. . . . 2nd ed. E.M. Murden & A. Ming, Jr., 4 Chambers St., New York, N.Y., 1827. 36 pp. [McDade no. 937].

BROADSIDES

Lines on the Murder of Mr. John Whipple, of Albany, Who was Shot Thro' the Window of his Dwelling, May 7th, 1827, by the Villanous Jesse Strang. 20 four-line stanzas. n.p., n.d. Woodcut of coffin marked Mr. J.W.

Farewell Address of Jessee Straang [sic] *to Mrs. Whipple.* 16 four-line stanzas. n.p., n.d. Two printings extant differentiated by last word, first line, second column. Tee changed to thee in what is, presumably, second printing. Other misspellings wo for woe, ma for may.

The Dying Words, Confession and Execution of Jesse Straang, [sic] *for the Murder of John Whipple, at Albany, August 27,* [sic] *1827.* 22 four-line stanzas. n.p., n.d. Woodcut of man on gallows.

NEWSPAPERS

Albany Argus, 1826-1827.

Freeman's Journal (Cooperstown), 1827

OTHER

*Blackburn, Roderic H. *Cherry Hill: The History and Collections of a Van Rensselaer Family.* Albany, N.Y.: Historic Cherry Hill, 1976.

Bonney, Catharina Van Rensselaer. *A Legacy of Historical Gleanings.* 2 vols. Albany, N.Y.: J. Munsell, 1875. Vol. 1, pp. 132 135.

*Mendel, Mesick, Cohen, Waite. *Cherry Hill Historic Structure Report* prepared for Historic Cherry Hill, revised 1981.

Strange, Charles A. "The Strangs of Westchester." *New York Genealogical and Biographical Record,* July, 1870. Vol. 101, no. 3, pp. 134-142.

*These two recent and excellent studies have been most useful in my revisions.

Index

122

124

Other Cherry Hill Publications

Cherry Hill: The History and Collections of a Van Rensselaer Family by Roderic H. Blackburn. 1976. 176 pages, 228 illus. "An irresistible combination of history, catalog, and picture book about the extraordinary house-museum Cherry Hill"—Charles Mudd. The starting point for anyone interested in reading about the house and its collections.

Hardcover ISBN 0-943366-00-3 *$15.00*
Softcover ISBN 0-943366-01-1 *$9.00*

Selected Receipts of a Van Rensselaer Family, 1785-1835 edited by Jane Carpenter Kellar, Ellen Miller, and Paul Stambach. 1976. 99 pages, 16 illus. Far more than a cookbook: a collection of recipes and remedies (how to bake a honey cake, brew beer, cure a toothache, etc.) from the handwritten copybooks of the Van Rensselaer family. Excellent for festive entertaining, living history programs, and browsing.

Softcover ISBN 0-943366-02-X *$5.00*

Selections from a Van Rensselaer Family Library, 1536-1799 edited by Joyce Jackson and Melissa Perlman. 1979. 17 pages. An annotated bibliography listing 41 books and pamphlets and 3 serial publications, reflecting the Van Rensselaer family's "tastes, ambitions, pursuits, and dispositions" (Preface).

Softcover ISBN 0-943366-03-8 *$2.50*

Not Just Another Pretty Dress: Two Centuries of Clothing and Textiles from Cherry Hill by Cornelia Frisbee Houde. To be published in 1983.

Softcover ISBN 0-943366-05-5 *Price not set*

Order from: *Historic Cherry Hill, 523½ South Pearl St., Albany, NY 12202.* Members discount 10%. Please add postage and handling charge of $1.30 for each *Cherry Hill* book and $1.00 for each other book ordered. Please add New York State sales tax if appropriate.